more is more

more is more

an antidote to minimalism

mary schoeser

conran
OCTOPUS

The seeds of this book were planted while working on an exhibition called *Decadence? Views from the edge of the century*, a show conceived by Louise Taylor at the Crafts Council Gallery in London. With our co-curator Philip Hughs, we set about to display the wide range of objects that, flying in the face of the fashion for minimalism, all radiated luxury, complexity or sensuality. The selection encompassed work that fitted comfortably with the 'craft' concept and some that did not: a cornucopia construction from moss and trash by the ceramicists Martin Moore and Janice Tchalenko, for example, and Andrew Logan's hanging, rotating, mirror-mosaiced sculpture, *Icarus*.

The theme binding this diversity was that elaborate, intricate and sophisticated objects often evoke nature, whether Mother Nature or human nature. The items focused attention on essential issues: life, death and eternity, past and present, hopes and fears. Real or imagined people were everywhere, depicted, reflected, suggested. Energy and flamboyance indicated an awareness of the precarious balance between a nature that must be protected and one that must be rejected.

It was a short step from thinking about objects in the gallery to thinking about interiors. In the anti-minimalist mood of these avant-garde exhibitors lay the seeds of a rebellion against the absence of things. Things are the substance of interiors and the evidence of human inventiveness and complexity; interiors themselves are often private galleries. Minimalism in this context seemed too elitist to satisfy any need but to exit the twentieth century on a determinedly 'modern' note. Minimalism has been pursued, as the British cabinetmaker John Makepiece put it, 'at the expense of function, expression and delight'. For him, Modernism's rich vocabulary has been worn out, used up, in the pursuit of minimalism.

The surroundings in which I interviewed exhibitors were highly individual. Makepiece, for example, lives next door to his workshop and school in an Elizabethan moated manor house; inside is a comfortable and stimulating mixture of old oak and a wide-ranging collection of modern furniture and art. A modern white-walled, open-plan, loft-type space, on the other hand, had been rendered by Logan into a visual feast. I could go on. What struck me was that none was 'fashionable'. Not one was minimalist. What they shared was being both timely and somehow timeless at the same time. Here was the richness of vocabulary that early Modernists deployed, even though the catchphrase for that 1920s' and 1930s' style was Ludwig Mies van der Rohe's 'less is more'.

Now, freed by the new century from the need to prove we are modern, it is clear that interiors have been moving towards something organic, equally at ease with past and present, equally concerned with global issues, such as renewable resources, and thoroughly private ones – biological and social responses, memories, personal identities, pastimes and passions. The following chapters explore these subjects in not a 'how-to' but a 'why-to' way, exposing the processes at work in the belief that the more you know, the more satisfying your interiors will be.

> *Minimalism is an overdose of artful emptiness.*
>
> Statement by Michelle Ogundehin, Deputy Editor, *ELLE Decoration*, for 'Decadence?' exhibition script, London: Crafts Council Gallery, Jan–Mar 1999.

opposite The rich visual vocabulary of original Modernists can be seen in this London home, which Ernö Goldfinger designed and built in 1939.

the language of interiors

Over the past thirty years, popular culture has become a subject of serious study. Historians, anthropologists, sociologists and linguists, among others, have contributed to a widely held belief that culture (the meanings by which we live) is revealed by the objects we admire, use, display or discard. Although varied in their exact theoretical starting point, all share an interest in the way objects communicate meanings.

Words fail us at crucial moments; we are unable to express the turmoil of inner thoughts that threaten to overwhelm us, so we resort to ancient modes of physical intimacy to express what we cannot or dare not say aloud.

Robin Dunbar, **Grooming, Gossip and the Evolution of Language** (London: Faber and Faber), 1996

Interiors are full of objects, but differ from what we wear, eat or read in generally existing over a much longer period of time. Few are created 'from scratch' and even these seldom remain unchanged. Evolving with us, they are places of both privacy and sharing, solace and celebration. They offer a chronicle of our lives.

opposite Through a potpourri of colours, materials, shapes and images we record our memories, ideas and aspirations.

gossip and grooming

If objects 'spoke', our homes would say a great deal. Since few of us design the structures we live in, the first thing our rooms reveal is our ability to compromise. They also reveal our natural inventiveness. The desire to decorate is found around the world and through time, as is the ability to take something intended for one purpose and use it for another. These human traits would have less value if we were unable to remember and share our inventiveness. This is, in part, what interiors do for us; they carry memories of our own activities, as well as the evidence of previous lives, both known to us and far distant and past.

The furniture we live with varies from culture to culture, but in each instance it has changed little in the past 500 years. In the Western world between 1500 and 1600 the castles or fortified manor houses of the nobility gave way to more sociable houses, intended for entertaining guests. Furniture gradually became less portable and multi-functional; in place of chests, stools, lightweight trestle tables and portable hangings came large tables and highbacked chairs, sideboards with plate racks, settles for storage and seating. Decorative plate (both pewter and silver), glass, ceramics and cutlery served for use and ornament. Bedrooms with bedside tables and chests of drawers evolved. Although lower down the social scale these changes were expressed in simpler materials or with fewer objects, the basic ingredients of today's interiors are recognizable by the 1550s.

above Some of the most sumptuous of 1630s interiors survive in Ham House, near London. There the long-established human desire for richly orchestrated details can still be seen at firsthand.

above Beds have been a focus of decoration for centuries, even when the materials used were humble woods, linen ticking and paint, as in this northern European boxbed of the eighteenth century.

left In his ancestral home, Longleat, built in 1567–79, the Marquess of Bath continually updates his private interiors by painting and collaging the walls.

What has changed since then is the styling of interiors, but more in the matter of details than of function. The major changes occurred slowly. It was not until the late seventeenth century for example that seating developed fixed padding and upholstery. Fabric and blinds first supplemented and then began to replace wooden shutters only 150–200 years ago.

This gradual process suggests not disinterest but rather satisfaction, tempered by the inventiveness of human nature. Despite the development of open-plan houses and studios, we still remain wedded to certain conventions. In both the East and West, a meal is extra-special if it is eaten at a table; a shelter is 'home' only if decorated, however simply. The patterns of behaviour tied to such conventions as these link us across time and space. They resonate for us in ways that are largely unconscious; our cultural memories are given visual expression through objects and the way we choose to use and arrange them.

The slow pace of change also suggests that the rooms we inhabit today cannot be radically new. Aside from certain furniture forms, the contribution to interiors of personal travels and exotic imports can be traced back to the sixteenth century. Today we are still revising our interiors around inventions of major importance in the twentieth century: the introduction of electricity supplies and the evolution of telecommunications, such as telephone, radio or television. The internet is simply the latest method of bringing information into our homes by electromagnetic means.

Yet interiors at the dawn of the twenty-first century have a look about them that makes them distinctly of their time. In a

below The laid table, warming hearth and ornamented mantle are all widely recognized signs of a stable and welcoming home. Such a personal selection of objects set within a traditional format puts people at their ease.

world now linked by the internet, the urge to create highly individual, even eccentric, interiors is on the increase. It is as if we are looking for an interior reality to tame the alarming effects of globalization. 'No', our interiors say, 'we are not all the same.' This impulse, though, again has roots in the far-distant past.

The universal message of interiors is that they are places to meet and create in. They also offer safety beyond the obvious physical barriers of walls and doors. Robin Dunbar, whose words open this chapter, is a developmental geneticist who argues that language emerged in humans to replace the grooming activity of our nearest relatives, the great apes. Grooming, in the form of cleaning or combing each other, is their way of establishing bonds, which then determine who will help out in a crisis. Dunbar believes we use language in the same way, to develop the relationships and loyalties that bind together the 'small world' of people that we depend on: those we can turn to for favours, advice, assistance and sympathy. Everywhere our small world numbers about 150 people, which is also, interestingly, the average size of a four-generational family. But without kinship links of this quantity, how do we form our clans? What if objects also play a part in creating and remembering bonds? Then how we decorate takes on a new significance.

The importance of the table and the visible signs of individuality in interiors provide direct links to those important activities of gossip and grooming. The 'gossip', or informal, personal conversation about persons or incidents that forms alliances, seems to be more confidential when shared inside around more formal board room, dining-room or restaurant tables. The 'grooming', a sensuous, touch-based form of bonding, is offered to family and friends in a ritual event each time they enter your home. After the warm greeting, the multitude of interior textures (and with them, colours) take over, sending their clues to the senses continually. Friends and allies will respond positively. If you point out a new vase or a newly painted

wall and, in compatible surroundings, their response will be to touch it. If others are content amid the contents of our homes, they are likely to be content with us, too.

above Displays of useful crockery – part of our interior vocabulary for at least five centuries – inevitably create a uniquely personal statement.

overleaf Persian or tribal rugs, vivid pigments and brightly dyed fabrics are so much at home in the West that we no longer think of them as 'foreign'.

Decorating, then, is not a trivial pursuit. Representing the anthropologist's point of view, Mary Douglas declared that 'good taste' is an index of social connections, reproductive fitness and our ability to mobilize resources. My own view is that the way this index of 'good taste' varies from place to place all over the globe is explained by the small-world theory. We need only understand and partake in the tastes of our own 'clan'; in decorating our homes we participate in preserving and adjusting that style. Doing so declares our allegiances. Doing nothing sends a message of disinterest in worldly connections, which is why the bare interior is rightly associated with hermits and religious orders. Clearly the common urge to make a room one's own is more than an indulgence; it may be a matter of survival.

fashions and fads

There is a cliché that claims that imitation is the sincerest form of flattery. We tend to discount the phrase because it has been said so many times, but for a condensed account of how fashions and fads develop, it can hardly be bettered. As to who we imitate, that is another matter.

In the mid-twentieth century the fashionable explanation was the 'trickle-down' theory, proposing that tastes were established by the wealthy and gradually adopted by everyone else in a form that they could afford. Although both our own experience and later theorists tell us this is generally not the case, this concept sparked off a debate about how we engage with architecture, design, advertising and the media. In today's global economy there is an insatiable appetite for information about how we develop a liking for one product over another. Clothing trends hold useful clues, especially the rise of 'street style'. 'Tribes' identify with each other through distinct elements of their dress, which can then 'trickle up', as occurred when punk-inspired garb appeared in the 1970s collections of London-based designer, Zandra Rhodes. In the 1990s street styles often depended not just on a particular look, but allegiance to a specific brand, indicated by a logo. Emerging from this phenomenon is the current belief in the power of 'branding', or developing a 'personality' for a company, even if what it sells is information or a service.

High fashion, on the other hand, is rife with ready-made personalities. Kept financially afloat on the sea of perfume and cosmetics that are sold under license, big-name fashion designers have on occasion turned their hands to interior products, too. In the 1980s Calvin Klein promoted a country-club look, more lately subdued into minimalism. Versace's recent collection has the verve and clash of the garments that earned the Italian designer cult status, combining interior products that range from throws

right Versace's 2000 home collection; vivid colours mixed with classical- and animal-inspired details can also be found in mid-twentieth-century home magazines.

far right The contrasting hues found in nature can provide constant inspiration, as can the advertisements depicting them.

inspired by wild animal-skins to classically patterned printed cushions. But does this account for the current fad for faux-skins in interiors? Probably not. It is equally likely to be the result of the continuing concern for endangered species, which has expressed itself in other ways, most notably in advertising (see the Benetton advertisement below). It may also be a revival style, forming part of the current fascination for mid-twentieth-century interiors. As this mixture of possibilities reveals, the slowly

evolving character of interiors makes them more resistant to the faddish influences from the fast-moving worlds of fashion, advertising and branding.

When you think about it, except for electrical goods there are few brands of influence in interiors. The reluctance to embrace brands within our homes is underscored by the fact that Dulux paints are widely known only because it is one of the most extensively 'branded' products of any kind, with millions invested in advertising annually. No other interior product has the equivalent backing, although Martha Stewart's style might be compared to a brand. A combination of extensive broadcasting, writing and promotion *has* made her a force to be reckoned with in the USA. Stewart's influence was so dominant in the 1990s that

Sunshine, my only SUNSHINE,
You make me happy HAPPY
When skies are grey.
You'll never know, dear,
How much I love you,
So please don't take
My sunshine away.

GLINT

GLISTEN

SUNGLASSES on G

NEW MENS CASUALWEAR COLLECTIONS DEPT.
NOW OPEN on LG 2

it even had an impact on the titling of books about interiors. Where once 'how to' or 'style' was an expected element of a title, Sharon Hanby-Robie went so far as to call her 1998 book *My name isn't Martha but I can decorate my home: the real person's guide to creating a beautiful home easily and affordably.* Never was there a clearer call for individual tastes. Yet we seem to do this naturally – when it comes to expressing our private persona, we are far more inclined to assemble an eclectic selection of furniture, ornaments, paints and patterns.

Inundated as we are with advertisements, there is ample evidence showing that we nevertheless choose our belongings as a result of personal experience, and the recommendations of our friends. Product promoters now speak of the 'anatomy of buzz'. An unlikely partner in this new word-of-mouth way of marketing is an increasing understanding of how epidemics spread. The 'buzz' book on this topic is Malcolm Gladwell's *The Tipping Point.* What it argues is that social epidemics (that is, fashions, attitudes, or behaviours) spread like viruses. The carriers of current 'viruses' – sushi, kitchens, dark-wood floors and organic living among them – are not infected, but infectious: sociable, energetic, knowledgeable or influential. In parallel with the small-world theory, it takes only some 150 people to start a social epidemic. In the world of interiors we might expect these to be found among decorators, magazine editors and stylists, but the list is in fact much longer than that.

One 'decorating epidemic' currently in vogue is multi-minimalism, or the use of identically shaped chairs, glasses, and many other objects, each in a different colour. It has all the hallmarks of a street style, developed out of ever-changing approaches within retail design and promotion – concepts that are equally valid for the sale of interior products as for any other type of product. Examples are common, extending from the entrancing temptation of a display of plain silk scarves in a range of different shades to the more recent appearance of the iMac computer packaged in five defining colours. This new, distinctive branding has revived Apple Macintosh's flagging fortunes and signalled the growth of trendy computer products, with their colours giving them a sharp edge over their utilitarian-style beige and grey contemporaries. Matching computer and desk accessories that quickly became available, and soon there were organic-looking, coloured-metal loudspeakers from Bang & Olufsen to complete the set. Even if you were not planning to buy a new system, magazine spreads appeared urging spray painting to 'fix' plain monitors.

The success of the iMac lay in the way that it tapped into an already existing taste. Consider how many mail-order catalogues photograph a particular item in all its colour variations. The original marketing impetus was to show all the possibilities; then it was used imaginatively throughout the 1990s by window dressers and, latterly, in interior magazines as well. Enough influential people, those 'carriers' of taste, took such displays literally, and took the notion home, to make it today a recognizable feature of our interiors.

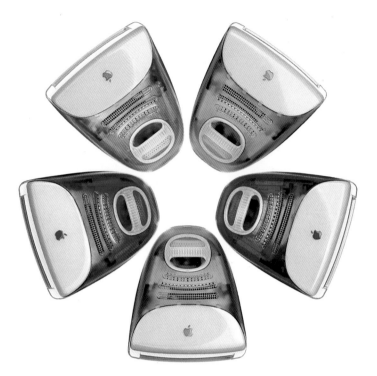

Collect all five.

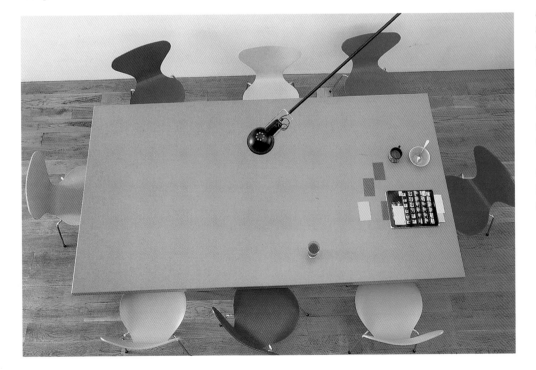

above Initially intended solely to show the range of hues available, 'multi-minimalist' product presentations such as this Apple Macintosh advertisement, show how utiliarian objects are transformed by the use of colour.

left Various colours for the table and Arne Jacobsen 'Series 7' chairs, designed in the mid-1950s and still in production, transform a potentially dull setting into a multi-minimalist delight.

far left Shop-window designers, as here at Harvey Nichols in London, continually provide new ideas for arranging and embellishing your interiors.

above *Upstairs, Downstairs* is still screened; it and other well-designed television programmes offer endless details to spark your own ideas.

right The drama of a formally dressed table is enhanced by the glints and shadows created by the lighting and candles.

Those tastemakers trawl widely for new sources of inspiration. Television and film are often influential. Past, present and future are all on offer, and often a response to a set design sparks off a trend. The acclaimed *Upstairs, Downstairs*, a London Weekend Television production that has had more than 60 million viewers worldwide since it was introduced in 1971, is one of a handful of long-running period dramas with an attention to detail that seems to have contributed to the wider adoption of particularly sumptuous table settings for special occasions. In modern vein the brightly coloured kitchen shelves seen around the world since 1994 in *Friends* lack doors and so reveal a vivid array of tightly packed packaging, endorsing this style. Even unlikely sources can be seen to have had their impact. Flowing from the success of *Blade*

Runner in 1982 were not only the later futuristic films enacted in apocalyptic settings seemingly cobbled together from found objects, but also the several variants of interiors that toyed with the same themes: industrial products put to new uses, rough-hewn 'unfinished' surfaces, and unexpected combinations of old and new.

It is only in seeing for ourselves that we make our own judgements. The appeal of a window display, film interior or friend's home is seldom wholesale. It is in the details that we recognize a 'fit' with some aspect of our own reality. There is no need for the intermediary of words; the attraction of a particular pattern, shape of chair or grouping of objects need not be explained, simply acknowledged. Imitation this may be, but melded into our own, entirely different, setting, the result is inevitably something unique.

handmade in the machine age

The epitome of machine-age production was the Model-T Ford, famously available in any colour as long as it was black – Henry Ford democratized consumption by narrowing choice. As standardization increased, individualized interiors made greater use of the handmade. Today's worldwide digital communications have extended our options over one-hundred fold. This might suggest that the handmade aspect of rooms is no longer of such importance. Not so. Both ever-increasing mass-production and globalization gradually put great power in the hands of corporations. France's leading dissident intellectual, the sociologist Pierre Bourdieu, has recently attacked this trend as 'market triumphalism'. The danger, he argues, is less regard for the environment, collectives and individual social rights. Even within the world of big business dissenters are emerging. One is Robert B. Reich, who, writing in the autumn of 2000 about 'The Choice Fetish' had this to say: 'Choices are supposed to be liberating. "Freedom of choice" is the economist's favorite topic, the libertarian's ideal, the classic liberal's alternative to revolution. But are we in danger of overdoing it?' Too many small choices, he contends, divert us from the big issues.

Reality is nonconformist. We live in a machine age, and yet we *live* in buildings that are, to a large degree, handmade. They may consist of and contain machine-made elements, but their assembly is still dependent on human intervention. Increasingly this aspect of interiors has been celebrated, and with good reason.

And what has all this to do with interiors? A great deal. As products of human skills, rooms and their contents record and recall the past as the site of human effort, they express in the present moment the ideal – joy in human labour – and shape the future. It is critical to make the distinction between the really important and not-so-important things. Reconsidering that soon-to-be-discarded piece of furniture, thinking inventively about recycling unlikely items, looking for materials that have been made in an eco-friendly way and supporting makers of individual objects bought at a fair price wherever they work, are all ways to shape and promote a better future.

These are not new ideas. What is new is their more frequent expression in interiors, and a growing awareness that the choices made by decorators, interior designers, architects and individuals can make a difference. An example of this is the inclusion of Daniel Quinn (alongside such well-known designers as Eames Demetrios, of the Eames Office, and Michael Vanderbyl, the award-winning San Francisco furniture, interior and graphic designer) as a 1999 cover story in *IS Magazine*, an American-based periodical detailing interiors and sources for professionals. Quinn was granted this accolade on the strength of his writing, primarily his 1991 novel, *Ishmael*. Winner of that year's Turner Tomorrow Award, an ecologically minded prize worth $500,000,

above Purchasing handmade objects from makers paid a fair price, where ever they work, is a practical way to build a better future and to personalize your home.

left 'Icon 20' is the surprising result of recycling: a Beidermeier sofa transformed by Alessandro Mendini, an influential member of Milan's Studio Alchimia, founded in 1976.

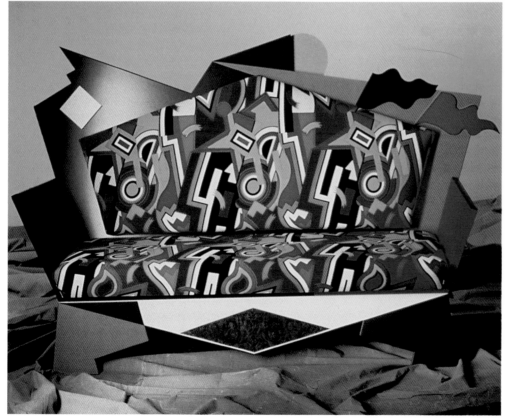

and now published in some 20 languages worldwide, its narrator is a 'student' taught by a gorilla. Through this character Quinn lays out a philosophy evolved since the mid-1970s, exposing the irrational myth within Western culture that demands catastrophic growth while assuring us that our habitat can absorb the consequences. While it might seem that the 'more-is-more' style is an inducement to consume thoughtlessly, in fact it engages directly with these very concerns, positioning recycled, retrieved, low-cost and energy-efficient objects centre stage. Minimalism is a much more expensive style to create, and to maintain.

Recycled and retrieved objects come in an astonishing diversity, from fine antiques to junk and items made from the leftovers of other types of manufacture. Trawling for secondhand treasures is an age-old sport; in the 1920s and 1930s it was the mainstay of the popular, and essential, 'new poor' style. What is new is the lack of economic need for many who partake in today's liking for curious cast-offs. Demand is so great that the price of junk, according to one source, rose tenfold during the past decade. This may account for the ever-widening categories of secondhand objects being brought into interiors, so that what not so long ago was called 'shabby chic' has become more adventurous. Melanie Molesworth's bluntly titled *Junk Style* in 1998, summed up this new change in mood.

Glass and paper are among the materials that are a long-established part of the recycling process, but in many cultures cast-off segments of wood, rubber, metal, acrylics and other

above Eco-friendly products need not be dull, as proved by the sumptuous fabrics laser-patterned by hand by Britain's Janet Stoyel.

opposite Recycling centres provided many of the pencils used by mosaic artist Jason Mercier for the hallway of Jaina Davis's Victorian home in San Francisco.

materials have traditionally been harvested for the production of handmade small carvings, candlesticks, picture frames and the like. Today this principle goes further. Take the vividly patterned coiled baskets made by artisans in Zimbabwe; since palm fibre, their traditional medium, has become scarce, they instead use switchboard cables to create bowls of wire. For those in search of such items, labelling has improved and fair-trade organizations exist in most countries to advise on appropriate sources and products. There is something to be said, too, for supporting makers closer to home; apart from the possibility that you may buy from a newly founded workshop and find in a decade that you have acquired a museum-quality piece, you can be guaranteed that your purchase will make a direct contribution to the maker's standard of living and continued creative growth.

The issue of low-cost and energy-efficient decorating is a minefield. Things that look simple may not be eco-friendly. White sheets are thoroughly bleached in the making, and this, together with some textile dyes, creates damaging waste. Look instead for 'green' fabrics, such as Sally Fox's cottons tinted in the growing by mulching in natural colouring fertilizers or throws and rugs from handharvested and handspun wools, naturally coloured silks or unusual fibres – horsehair, nettle, hemp, Columbian *Calotropis procera* – that provide a viable living elsewhere. While these fibres yield soft-toned products, low-waste processes need not give dull results, as demonstrated by the scintillating laser-patterned lengths handproduced by Janet Stoyel in rural Devon.

Nevertheless, when in doubt, do it yourself. This at least reduces the chance that harmful glues, pigments, bleaches and cleansers will be used. It also opens the door to the exploration of unusual recycling treatments: walls covered with leftover paper and wood products, coffee-table bases made from discarded containers (washing-machine drums have been used to good effect in this way), or vases and storage boxes culled from plastic, metal and cardboard packaging.

the artist's eye

Ever since 1917, when the French artist Marcel Duchamp attempted to place a urinal in a New York gallery and called it ready-made art, 'found' elements of domestic interiors have been fair game for those artists seeking to question the conventional meanings of both art and objects, and how we view them. Nevertheless, however radical or traditional the work, all skilled artists bring private feelings into the public domain. Interiors do something similar, though on a more intimate level.

The links between rooms and art have been increasingly obvious in the past two decades, as videos of performance artists and installations (that is, temporary arrangements of objects in a gallery context) have given permanence to these once-fleeting works. The most human-centred art form, performance, emerged during the 1960s, although its roots are in early twentieth-century movements, such as Futurism and Dada. In essence, it involves a playful blurring of the borderline between reality and art, making us aware of the artistic qualities of everyday life. While performances may occur outside, if live they always contain an element of 'interior', since viewers must be present in the same space and time, often in close proximity or even directly involved. Inside, the interior itself often plays a role in the performance. As for the participants, in their use of common but often stylized gestures, motions and poses, they parallel contemporary dancers, the difference being that the latter are choreographed and performance art, in principle, is not. Fashion catwalk shows contain similar stylizations. In all these cases we are invited briefly into a recognizable and yet imaginary world. Entering someone else's home, on the other hand, provides the same elements but with an opposite emphasis; the rooms are real yet, even so, almost always contain elements that represent the imaginary – the past, the future, other cultures.

The breakdown of boundaries between art forms has encouraged a reassessment of interiors and their contents. Again, this can be traced back to the previous century, and even further.

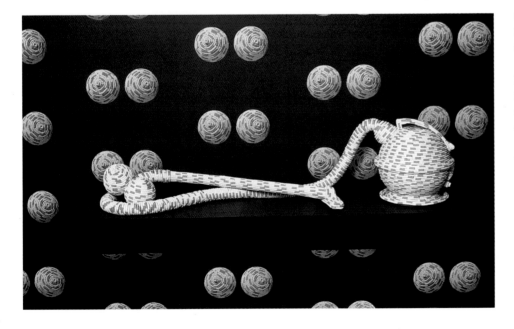

above The sculptor Nina Saunders toys with traditional furniture forms; in her mid-1990s bulging Chesterfield she lampoons gentlemen's clubs that exclude women.

left The breakdown of barriers between art forms has reawakened a surrealistic interest in both junk and domestic things; here Sarah Lucas used cigarettes to create a vacuum cleaner.

far left Fashion collides with furniture in Hussein Chalayan's 'lamp table' skirt, part of his Winter 2000 catwalk collection.

The lively painted and patterned interior surfaces and objects of the Omega group, who were active in London during World War I epitomize these earlier trends, but they were created, on the whole, by a limited number of people, generally artists. With the arrival of Post-modernism this began to change. Robert Venturi, an American architect, influenced this through his building, furniture and fabric designs. Without using the actual term Post-modernism, he summarized it in written form as 'complexity and contradiction in architecture'. His now widely used definition could apply equally to architecture, art or interiors that contain 'elements which are hybrid rather than "pure", ambiguous rather than "clear", conventional rather than "designed", accommodating rather than "excluding"'. Post-modernism thus opened the way for domestic appliances and furniture to be designed or reassessed as if they were works of art, and for artists to employ them as subjects for their own investigations.

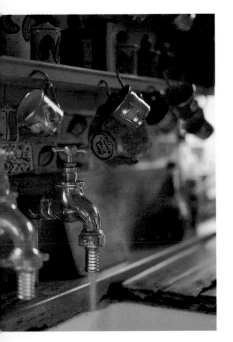

above The daily use of casually arranged storage tins and handpainted mugs creates a visually complex and ever-changing display.

right With ingredients as simple as scraps of fabric, glue and staples, an interior can be transformed, in this case for an October 2000 *World of Interiors* fabrics feature.

Much leading-edge art since the early twentieth century has been sculpture or, later, its related form, installation. As part of this trend, two of the larger interior objects – seating and folding screens – have offered up their sculptural and conceptual possibilities to both artists and designers. Duchamp's first 'ready-made' piece of 1913 was, tellingly, a stool with a bicycle wheel fixed above it by means of a fork. Since then seating has experienced many new forms, a phenomenon that is well documented. However inspired, whether by Bauhaus philosophy, principles of ergonomics and engineering, or the plot of a film, the new materials used for seating often led the way to the wider

acceptance of metals, plastics and other nontraditional substances in interiors. At the same time these various influences produced radical changes in the shape and weight of furniture. Seeking to change perceptions rather than use, sculptors such as Nina Saunders have played with traditional forms of furniture. Her bulging mid-1990s Chesterfields, for example, take the world of gentlemen's clubs, whisky and power into another realm, as she questions, as a woman artist, 'the kind of places where decisions are made, and that you have no access to'. The recent revival of leather-covered, deep-buttoned ottomans and sofas, sometimes made 'edgier' by metal studs, gives us an opportunity to make our own statement on similar issues, in our own homes.

In contrast to seating, the folding screen has remained more faithful to its basic form. Instead this ancient element of interiors was 'reinvented'. Once painters depicted it as suggesting both explicit and implied meanings through its ability simultaneously to reveal and hide, or alternately emphasize and divert attention. Today it has become an object recognized by artists as capable of expressing their perceptions directly, and examples can be found in modern galleries and museums around the world. The screen's revival also further reveals the collapse of boundaries; the screen of undulating moulded plywood and canvas made as a piece of furniture by Charles Eames in 1946 (and now in the Museum of Modern Art, New York) is as satisfyingly sculptural as the giant glass-and-steel screen-installation, *Wave Wall*, created by Danny Lane in 1993. The question, 'Is it art or furniture?' matters little in terms of the influence such pieces have had on mainstream interiors. They remind us of the movability of furniture and the human liking for creating intimate spaces within larger ones, and thus the constantly shifting strategies we apply to make our interiors our own personal statement.

In radical instances, such as Gregor Schneider's *Dead House ur*, in Rheydt, Germany, an entire house has been transformed over a period of fifteen years, with the removal and return of

portions of the interior. Behind the anonymous facade this project explores things that escape perception – substances, spaces, objects and qualities that remain hidden behind a labyrinth of interior walls and floors. This is a performance-interior at its most conceptual. If you are tempted to think that *Dead House ur* is a fairly isolated example, one far removed from everyday interiors, then there are ample reasons to think again. The representation of such performance-interiors is predominantly by photographs, which is of course the very same vehicle that magazines depend upon. High-style fashion photography is recognized as an art form in its own right, building on and reinforcing the theatricality of a catwalk show. High-style interior photography struggles, still,

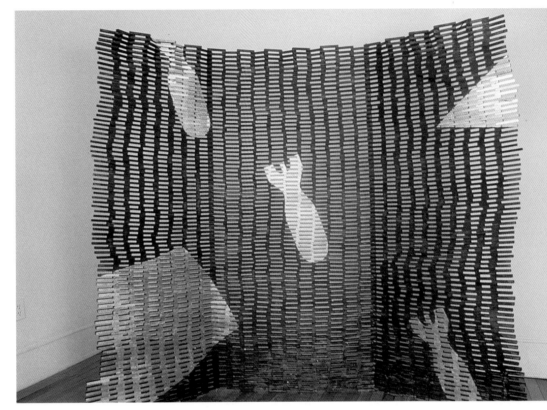

to achieve the same status, caught between the need to be seductive and yet informative to its audience. The solution? One is to find interiors that have plenty to say, a strong visual style that expresses the personality of their owners. Another is to make the most of the editorial pages that highlight new products and style trends, by juxtaposing a myriad of objects. By showing these, magazine photographers and art editors have exposed us to a variety of possible attitudes to rooms, from sources all around the world. In search of the idiosyncratic, they have lately presented the magazine-reading public with interiors stripped of old wallpaper but not redecorated, rooms full of flaking plaster, mouthwatering close-ups of handpainted cups and crockery, stockpiles of rescued plaster ornaments and out-of-the-way houses that have few modern conveniences or furnishings. Rooms may be frozen in time, essentially untouched for decades and still stylish, or now-crumbling remnants of their former selves. 'Up to date' is evidently an attitude rather than a particular style; try

dipping into *Nest*, a magazine born in the USA in 1997, if you have any doubts.

Avant-garde magazines' atmospheric portrayal of interiors asks us to question what we accept as beautiful and how we interact with rooms and their contents. Our perceptions are challenged at a visual and a psychological level. Artists ask us to re-think the furniture and objects we often take for granted. At the same time, it is within their designs and through their interiors that concepts such as minimalism and modernism are encompassed, and made accessible for the public eye. What is more, the collage–like nature of decorating gives it the potential for constant revision and exploration. The tangible and conceptual – from colours and materials to ideas and obsessions – are our media, and it is these media that are explored in the following chapters.

above Washington DC sculptor, Mary Annelaa Frank, is one of a number of artists making screens; shown here is '24 Karat Fear', constructed during the Gulf War.

opposite The sculptural qualities of a 1950s' Harry Bertoia metal mesh 'Diamond' chair adds emphasis to the forms of the everyday things surrounding it.

colour

Minimalism is a restrained expression of Post-modernism: less is more.

The advocates of both have been equally inspired by a delight in

architectural motifs and their love of natural and

faux-natural materials. The textures and colours of

granite, gravel, glass, marble and wood featured

significantly in post-modernist interiors of the late

1980s and, in subdued shades, gave minimalists in

*Postmodernism is basically
characterized by the
rediscovery of ornament,
colour, symbolic
connections and the
treasure trove of the history
of form.*

V. Fischer (ed.), **Design Now: Industry or Art?**
(Munich: Pressstel-Verrlag), 1989

the 1990s the design capacity to highlight that single, well-chosen object

– a quirky sculpture, the designer chair, a clear vase containing a handful

of exotic blooms.

Given that the rich and eclectic elements of Post-modernism were at

the same time the roots of the minimalist style, it was therefore inevitable

that the days of the pared-down interior were numbered. The breakaway

began with colour.

opposite Colour, light and cast shadows work
together to accent objects, create atmosphere and
define the character of a room.

moving away from minimalism

The move away from a minimalist style towards more colour in the interior can be traced to diverse sources. The rethinking of historic interiors, the firsthand exploration of Mediterranean lifestyles, and changes in retailing and mail-order marketing tactics all played a significant part. Originating out of an art movement pioneered in the USA in the 1960s, Minimalism has evolved since then and colour has been the key to that change.

Minimalist artists aimed to reduce sculpture and painting to their essential forms. The major figures within this movement were Carl André, Donald Judd, Dan Flavin, Sol LeWitt and Robert Morris; symmetry, repetition and factory production were the key elements of their clean-edged works. A cerebral style, it rejected any evidence of the artist's hand or emotions; this aspect in particular made it an unlikely influence on interiors. The only truly minimalist interiors of the 1960s and 1970s were accidentally so: bland corporate waiting rooms, warehouses or factories.

By the 1980s minimalist art, especially the wall paintings of LeWitt and light works of Flavin, was moving on towards rich colour and surfaces and a more explicit sensuality and expressiveness. This was when a related interior style emerged – a 'high-tech' combination of brightly coloured rubber flooring, PVC walls, perforated metal shelving and seating, and the like. The impetus behind this style probably owed as much to Italians such as Etorre Sottsass,

above The colour choice offered in many household items can be used as a decorative feature; here glasses were selected to coordinate with the tiled tabletop.

opposite A light, contemporary touch is given to this set of Victorian chairs with upholstery in different toned plain silks.

an avant-garde designer of the late 1960s and 1970s who in 1981 co-founded the Memphis design group in Milan. Including designers from other European countries as well as Japan and the USA, Memphis, which disbanded in 1988, broadened the Italian interest in communicative, consumption-inducing design into an international style that adapted surface colours, patterns and shapes from any time or culture. In the process, its designers transformed furniture and other household products into eccentric objects akin to sculptures.

The word 'minimalism' was surprisingly only adopted in the 1990s as a term for an interior style. Although it was first used to describe a 1980s fashion trend, interiors embraced it more slowly. Both had a quality of absence. The look was conceptual, in keeping with both the original art movement and the work of Memphis. But new elements were introduced, such as the incorporation of irregular, handmade marks and a reduction of colour and artifice that expressed spiritualism over materialism and 'for ever' over 'now'. As a fashion concept it can be traced to the 1980s and Junicji Arai, Issey Miyake, Rei Kawakubo and a handful of other Japanese designers, whose understanding of their craft resulted in seemingly timeless textiles and garments that resounded with inventiveness and cultural expression. In general their effect rested on exploring and exposing the inherent qualities of a material's colour, texture and behaviour. Extrapolated into interiors of the mid-to late 1990s, this meant monochrome colour schemes – all white, all wood – with the texture and character of each material introducing a limited degree of relief. Strategically placed sculptural furniture and an object or two echoed in attitude, if not in style, the emphasis on form that had previously been popularized by Memphis.

The 1990s were not without colour altogether. In fact, a scan through *Elle Decoration* and other upbeat and innovative magazines of 1989–93 yields ample evidence of its use, in the years before the arrival of natural palettes and increasingly minimalist tastes. But the main proponents of the early 1990s vivid style were those already associated with high colour, such as Sally Brampton, editor of British *Elle*, the ceramicist Mary Rose Young, the couturier Lacroix (courtesy of his favourite interior designers, Garouste and Bonetti), television producer Trevor Hopkins (via

the artists and occasional decorators João Penalva and Michael Scott) and Paloma Picasso. Although featured in magazines, their rooms were private spaces, many of which 'went white' a few years later. Instead, the sustained influence on the adoption of colour trends in interiors, came from the architects and designers involved in the design of public spaces.

Hotels, for instance, having for decades appeared institutional in nature, changed dramatically over the course of the 1990s, moving towards a styling that was unique to the venue. The Paramount Hotel, off Broadway in New York, was one of the first. Almost certainly the most influential hotel refurbishment of 1990, the entire scheme was conceived by the French designer Philippe Starck, who elected in the lobby and mezzanine floor above it to scatter a large number of chairs and sofas, each one upholstered in one or two colours of plain velvet. Starck's use of a variety of colours in this manner created intimate groupings of furniture that brought an alluring and near-theatrical sense of impending tête-à-tête to these interiors. This approach undoubtedly set the seal of approval on richly toned and textured furnishings, which then gradually began to meld together previously separate trends – the modern and the historical. A hint of this fusion came in Starck's choice of seating in the Paramount; it was drawn, significantly, from several contemporary designers, rather than just one. This signalled a move away from the uniformity that had previously so often been found in the modern interiors frequented by the social and corporate elite.

Seating is so often the clearest statement of an interior's ambience, no matter what the style, and has been employed as such by those like Starck who applauded multiplicity rather than singularity. For celebrants of the 'more-is-more' style, chairs of

above A wallpainting and a chandelier (made from two photographic lampshades, toys and perspex balls) enliven an entry-way alcove turned dining room in the Wiltshire home of textile designers Leo Santos Shaw and Margrét Adolfsdóttir.

opposite New York interior designer Thomas Jayne used large rectangles of colour to define areas in his loft home.

virtually any period or material can be adapted to enrich rooms that might otherwise be severely minimalist or, at the other end of the spectrum, too perfectly of their period and therefore lacking a contemporary edge. Often, it is the casual but considered juxtaposition of several plain colours – and this alone – that makes the seating come to life. For those who admire mid-twentieth-century modernism, dining room chairs – by Arne Jacobsen, perhaps – might well be the same shape but, under the influence of multi-minimalism, they can be purchased in many different colours. Others, who cannot bear to part with that beloved set of Victorian rosewood chairs, but at the same time have no desire to recreate faithfully a nineteenth-century interior, should consider the light, humorous note that is sounded by upholstering the chairs in several different hues.

The intimacy and atmosphere created by juxtaposing one area of colour against another can be employed as a useful tool in interiors of all kinds. To provide focus, define one area from another, or simply add richness, the use of various colours has become a keynote of today's interiors. Drawing together various influences that have evolved over the past two decades, the ensuing result is not so much a new look as a new attitude, one that is emotional but at the same time grounded in a reality that encompasses both the history and science of pigments, with an understanding of human colour-related needs and responses, and with the transforming effect that colours have on an interior. The ease with which colour can be introduced into a room is part of its everlasting appeal, making it the first thing to coincide when it is time for change.

above A lively array of plates and glasses, and coloured cubes that echo the design of the chairs, add interest to a monochrome interior.

right Soft-toned cushions and painted panels in shades of grey provide a subtle richness, as in this Asian-influenced London interior.

above left Different-coloured bright slipcovers provide key accents, their solidity balancing and grounding the delicate wire chandelier.

the point about paint

There was a time not long ago when it seemed that the only 'right' way to make an interior fashionable was to paint every surface white. While distinctly modern in concept, in reality it was difficult to live with. Even the British fashion designer Jean Muir, who was well known for her all-white London home, also had a Northumbrian house full of colour and pattern. On a practical level, white marks quickly. The simple solution is to retouch, but there is the temptation of paint; it is so easy to use that it can be done often, and experimentally. If you don't like the result, then it can be painted over again.

There are other reasons why white is difficult to live with. For many people it is reminiscent of clinical or institutional surroundings, whether the hospital they associate with unpleasant memories, the classroom they

longed to flee or the impersonal office (though increasingly a thing of the past) in which individual touches were banned. White is a colour of deprivation. Our biological response, uncontrolled by the conscious mind, in an all-white cell is well documented: it drives us crazy. In the all-white natural environment, that relatively rare world produced only by a long and heavy snowstorm, the senses are disoriented as the eyes strain to find the horizon or a familiar roofline or tree.

Our biological responses and colour memories ensure that few domestic interiors are ever entirely white. They also determine to a great extent which colours we feel comfortable with; it is no surprise to find that many people choose to dress themselves and live among objects of similar hues. If uncertain about a new colour for a room, we can always try the colour of a favourite shirt or sweater. Even if this treasured garment seems an improbable starting point, it is likely that on the walls, its familiar hue will soothe with its personal resonances.

above Against a background of daubed, oil-based reds, the richness of unframed canvases is highlighted.

right A welcoming storage and display area is the result, when drawfronts are painted in a range of colours to enliven an old cabinet.

opposite A wall painted a water-based blue wall gives a relaxing glow in a sun-lit position.

colour

We often hesitate to use unusual colours in interiors because overlaid on our personal preferences are our learnt responses to colour. Red, for example, is universally symbolic of fire, life and passion. We are told that our biological response in a red room is an increase in blood pressure, perhaps because red in nature is often also a sign of danger, and we are unconsciously preparing for 'fight or flight'. We are also told that dark colours on the ceiling make it appear lower. Yet neither of these statements is entirely true. In my living room the ceiling is a soft, deep cherry red. It appears higher than it really is (because it is *bright* colours that make surfaces appear closer) and casts a rosy glow throughout the room. The result is a north-facing room that is warm and restful. An added bonus, appreciated by all my female friends, is the beneficial effect a reflected red has on skin tones.

right Draw on your artistic talents by painting or decoupaging simple images onto cabinet doors; varnished, they will withstand everyday use.

below Take inspiration from historical examples, such as this chair painted by Dante Gabriel Rossetti in 1856, now in the Victoria & Albert Museum, London.

Our individual likes and dislikes are in part shaped by the way we see colours. Descriptions of colours in old museum catalogues, in aged inventories or in today's databases make it clear that even specialists view colours in uniquely personal ways. Exact colour matching can only be obtained by recourse to means other than words (which is why paint charts and sample pots are so widely available). This is especially true for 'off' colours, anything that isn't a true red, green, blue, and so on. What is peach to one may well be apricot to another. In the end it matters very little which word is chosen, as long as the colour is the right one. Matt or gloss, perfectly rendered or daubed on, what makes it right may be any number of things: a reminder of a favourite flower, a memory of a room where we felt specially welcome, an evocation of the taste and smell of cooking in a kitchen frequented as a child.

The connection between food and colour is summed up in that single word, taste. We speak of bitter greens and tangy yellow-orange shades in subconscious awareness of the way in which colour can literally spice up our lives. In fact when seasonings and dyes were exotic imports to Europe from the East and West Indies, both were called spices. Today we have hundreds of paint colours to choose from, and no shortage of advice about which ones to pick, how to apply them, and whether to use one or several in the same room. If in doubt, our own taste in food can serve as a useful starting point. If colours were spices, the more mid-toned ones in a room, the richer and livelier the result. As for a strong colour, think of cumin, cinnamon or pepper. A little can make a big impact.

The wide range of paint effects and finishes now available is a result, in part, of the great interest in historical interiors over the past two decades. When the American Shaker furniture captured global imaginations, part of its appeal lay in how the simple, beautifully constructed chairs, chests and boxes were set against an interior with matt, rich, mid-toned painted walls or details – skirting boards, architraves around windows and doors, and the doors themselves. Other techniques were stenciling and dragged and daubed effects, inspired by interiors of other periods from around the world. Quick to sense the interest, specialist paint suppliers sprang into being and established suppliers broadened their off-the-shelf ranges.

If authenticity is the goal, today we can have Picture Gallery Red or Drainpipe Grey from Farrow & Ball, suppliers of specialist and traditional paints (the grey that of exterior ironwork at the UK's National Trust properties). Add character with William Morris Green from Fired Earth's range of colours, developed in tandem with the curators at the Victoria & Albert Museum, which, in honour of its spring 2000 exhibition on Art Nouveau, created ten more shades, taken from colours used by the movement's champions, Charles Rennie Mackintosh and Victor Horta. For the environmentally minded, mix-yourself casein milk paints – including gold, silver or bronze 'glimmer' – can be obtained from companies such as Nutshell Natural Paints. The same types of paints can replicate the rendering of age-old treatments in texture as well as colour, since they are inclined by their constituents and their consistency to variations in tone, coverage and thickness. If glazed, dragged or stippled effects appeal, there are also numerous variants of ready-mixed paints. Finally, if you are the owner of an old property and are really serious about discovering its early character, you can call on expert analysts of original paint, who, through minute scrapings of the walls, floors and original fittings, can reconstruct the original scheme. Aside from making a valuable contribution to the more accurate reconstruction and of historical interiors, their discoveries have revealed surprisingly vivid hues or seemingly unlikely colour combinations, which in turn has exposed us in a different way to the impact paints can make in defining a room's character.

For the adventurous, painting patterns on walls and even furniture has never been easier. Non-drip and low-odour water-based paints have revolutionized what was once a messy business. Not so long ago it would have been folly to aim to evoke the living room of

above Dyes and pigments, like condiments, were once rare and costly commodities; today endless colours are available to help you 'spice up' your interiors.

Edward Bawden, a twentieth-century English artist who used oil paints spread on corrugated cardboard and pressed to the walls to create an irregular stripe, or even the painted and lacquered wooden chairs decorated by the Pre-Raphaelite artist, Dante Gabriel Rossetti. Today it would be a pleasure. Whether working freehand, using stencils or masking tape, or exploring the textures and marks made by stamping with 'found' patterning devices, the result is guaranteed to be unique.

As the least expensive way to change a room completely in a day, paint and its many possibilities have become the starting point for many a new decorative scheme. Best of all, there is only one rule to remember. Whether buying ready-mixed or a custom colour, buy enough for the entire project and some retouching.

cultural hues

Intuition, context and emotion each drive our colour choices. Shaping these influences are cultural tendencies: ethnicity, geography and localized tastes all affect the way that we process colour. In India, for example, a rich shade of clear turquoise blue is said to be pleasing to the eye of God, while in other cultures, including those of Central America and Egypt, a darker ultramarine blue is associated with death. Elsewhere, such as among Native American Indians, turquoise is a talisman, granting strength and good luck; for many Europeans coral holds just the same meaning, a legacy from the sixteenth and seventeenth centuries, when privileged children were often given coral jewellery to ward off sickness.

The impact that colours have on us is closely connected to cultural memories, especially those related to spirituality and wellbeing. Colour and healing have a long association, which has lately received attention from seemingly opposing quarters. Eastern alternative medicine and living styles, such as feng shui, are in fact more or less in accord with Western studies of topics such as visual ergonomics and how colour triggers physical and chemical changes in the body. Blue and blue-tinged colours lower the heart rate and are calming; placed just in the sightline's periphery in a study, they induce concentration. Colours at the opposite end of the spectrum are instead enlivening but here is where biology and culture diverge. In the West, especially in urban areas, 'hot' reds, oranges and saffrons are expected to make people alert, even jumpy. Elsewhere these are deeply spiritual colours; there is the red of the Hindu Lord Kataragama, the saffron of Buddhist monks' robes. The animation these colours induce is expected to be of the sustained and focused kind. Gold, used to treat arthritis and long coveted as a substance and a colour, is simultaneously suggestive of the divine (as in halos) and earthly greed; in interiors it has lately made a comeback, often playing with this paradox. And car spray paints, it turns out, offer the best selection of gilt hues.

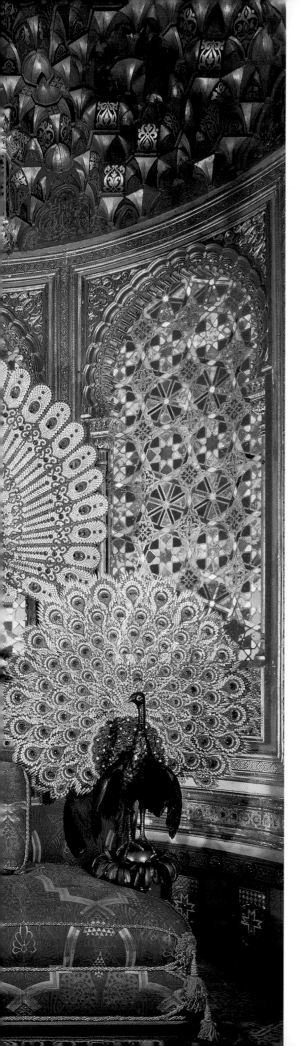

The seriousness of today's attitude to a healthy spirit and body cross over into travel for enlightenment and travel for sport, both of which in turn have done much to disperse cultural hues. Our childhood surroundings provide us with a starting point, yet we change our cultural responses to colour over time, just as we change our tastes in food. Spending time among the blue of the Brahmin houses of Jaipur in north India, the traditional Suffolk pink of many English East Anglian houses, or the dark primaries and powdery pastels that dot and decorate houses in Sydney and San Francisco alike, can alter our perceptions about the 'right' colours to live with.

These days we need not even travel to gain similar insights. Immigrant communities have overlaid their homeland's cultural hues over existing buildings and interiors. The globalization of architectural practices has also induced a wide use of once-localized palettes, most notably in the work of the Mexican Ricardo Legoretta, who follows his countryman Luis Barragán in using vibrant, saturated hues to charge architecture with emotion. The painted walls traditional to Mexican villages now adorn buildings around the world. And then there are the magazines, in which a typical issue might juxtapose interiors in Italy, New York, London's East End and Morocco, each echoing its distinctive surroundings yet revealing elements of cultural exchange in its use of colour, materials and pattern.

above Juxtaposing things from different cultures can provide striking contrasts, as in this Beirut interior, where a bentwood rocker and plaid throw are glimpsed through an intricate archway.

left The Moorish Kiosk, Linderhof, Germany, shows how bright mosaic-like treatments reinforce an exotic theme.

above Dark green is a calming colour and suggests verdant climates; in Lindesfarne Castle, Northumberland, England, this shade perfectly complements a seventeenth-century painted Dutch cabinet.

is wet or dry heat. In many arid climates inclinations run towards darker, 'mustier' hues. For example, incorporating what the interior designer Charles Riley called 'a new desert palette', *American Home* magazine's House of the Year 2000, in Las Vegas, contained cobalt blue blinds and wallcoverings in either vivid orange or a mottled bronze. My own desert-foothills childhood is partly what has constantly drawn me towards bricky oranges, azure-sky blues and piney greens, even when they were not easily available in furnishings and even though, in theory, they ought not to 'work' in my English home. When it comes to traditional colour combinations, some have fixed meanings when combined in a particular pattern. The clearest example is with tartans – wherever they are used they indicate Scotland and a powerful blend of strong clan bonds with a fierce independence of mind. Even the Burberry plaid (predominantly tan with cross-stripes of black, white and red) carries the same message, but transmuted into modern parlance: for clan read class, for independence of mind read independence from financial worries.

Climate and landscape are natural influences in interiors, despite the fact that most modern buildings are designed to keep the former out. Those who live away from their original culture often evoke its climate, recreating its impact in their new homes. In 1996, in the midst of minimalism, the Paris-based fashion-trade show organizer Maria Lucia Gamboa Caycedo explained her deep rose, pink, lime and gold candlelit bedroom as the result of her Colombian childhood: 'heat, sunshine, salsa and the South American temperament'. But heat and sunshine in one part of the globe does not necessarily suggest a single palette of colours. Much depends on whether it

There are less rigidly defined combinations that nevertheless suggest a type of culture, if not a specific location. In the developed world combinations within one object of lots of small areas of different, pure colours brings to mind folk art and thus other cultures. Displaying such an arteface can suggest bohemianism, an unconventional lifestyle or, at least, a yearning for it. If instead, the desired effect is permanence and timelessness, it can be brought into an interior by deep red and yellow ochres, golden earth tones and black used together, particularly with wood, earthenware or metal objects. They suggest antiquity, and with good reason, since these are the most plentiful and easily obtained natural colours, often derived from the raw materials themselves. Such colour combinations occur throughout the history of decorative arts and cut across class and regional boundaries, appearing in Aboriginal art, Samurai armour, Middle Eastern and Iberian wall and floor treatments, and that same Burberry plaid.

above Mixtures of blues and terracottas evoke easy-going, warm places, especially when they are handpainted in a naive style.

left Different textures have cultural messages, too, as can be seen in this rough-hewn, Masai-type interior, decorated with smooth and gleaming European fittings.

Given our strong personal preferences for colours and, in turn, the impact they can have on us, we tend to use them for interior accessories rather than more permanent features, such as furniture, tiles or cabinetry. This said, the latter are today available in a full range of shades and decorative treatments, providing ample choice of colour and hue for the bold hearted. There is however, no sure-fire formula for success. Given that this is the case, there are numerous ways to try out other cultural hues before committing them to an interior scheme. Wrapping papers, covered notebooks and embroidered, printed and stitched handbags, scarfs, sari lengths and shawls are manufactured and available all over the world. They provide a quick means of testing an effect and colour, and, as a bonus, can eventually be used for their original purpose, too.

colour cacophony

Nature abounds with colour, mixed in subtle and vibrant combinations, and changing with the time of day, the weather and the seasons. It teaches us much of what we take for granted as 'rational' colour schemes. In Minimalism, especially its white-on-white form, we had a style that feared colour, as if it might corrupt or contaminate us. The opposite – the confident indulgence in colour in all its manifestations – might well be dubbed cacophonous, not so much because it might sometimes be discordant, but to underline the lack of agreement it suggests. Dissonance often encourages personal individuality; colour cacophony does, too.

below White furniture can be 'tinted' by lighting; a changing array of colours creates a dramatic effect in the bar of the St Martins Hotel, London, designed by Philippe Starck.

The connection between sound and colour is that both are identified by us through their different wavelengths. Establishing this in the mid-nineteenth century, the German philosopher Goethe proposed that certain colour combinations would be harmonious. The problem with this theory, as the spread of the world's music has taught us, is that different tonal arrangements inevitably appeal to different cultures. These cultures might even be on our doorsteps. Rock and roll was originally resisted as 'just noise' by traditionalists who feared its debasing and corrupting impact; chromophobics in Western cultural and intellectual movements have resisted colour in a similar way. In a recent study of this topic David Batchelor outlines the many and varied attempts to purge colour, either by making it the property of some 'foreign' body – the Oriental, the feminine, the infantile, the vulgar or the pathological – or alternatively by relegating it to the realm of the superficial, the supplementary, the inessential or the cosmetic. So be it. This makes colour cacophony all the more

above Shadows add interest to an interior – here natural light creates a pattern on a flat wall.

opposite Nooks, crannies, steps and ledges are thrown into relief in Andrew Logan's London home/studio, by a combination of shadows and changes in colour.

appropriate for our times, which celebrate 'otherness' as much as self, and the small things that make life fun as much as the large things that make life better.

The abundance of nature is inextricably bound to both conscious and unconscious notions of the female. Perhaps this accounts for the fact that professional colourists are frequently women. Tricia Guild of Designer's Guild is often called the doyenne of colour, and rightly so; her company has promoted adventurously coloured textiles and interiors for more than a decade. Her recently redecorated London home combines lapis slashed with emerald and fuschia, and the iron rails of the central staircase are an assertive tangerine. Jill Pilaroscia, a San Francisco-based artist turned colourist, advises on product and interior schemes for clients including Herman Miller, Hewlett-Packard, and Skidmore, Owings & Merrill. Pilaroscia is in part responsible for the growing belief that the workplace should express joy and embody enthusiasm – in other words that it should support the positive aspects of human nature.

Links between nature and womanhood underpin the writings of Camille Paglia, whose 1990 work on sexual personae, art and decadence has contributed to the revived use of the word decadence since then. As a figure of speech, decadence has a present-day currency partly drawn from history: the 'divine decadence' of Sally Bowles was being played out in *Cabaret* on the New York stage not long ago, while *Les Misérables* in London continues to retell Victor Hugo's 1862 tale of revolution, in which the fictitious Jean Valjean declares: 'dry happiness is like dry bread. We eat, but we do not dine. I wish for the superfluous, for the useless, for the extravagant, for the too much, for that which is not good for anything.' Minimalism simply is unable to offer a similar feeding ground.

Colour cacophony is not solely the province of women, though. Tom Dixon, Habitat's Head of Design UK, has, for instance, recently created a range of brightly enamelled steel Ts

and Ds for the David Gill New Gallery in London; these building blocks are for self-assembly of anything one can make from them. As this

above Strong colours underpin Gabhan O'Keefe's witty take on early eighteenth century styles in Säo Schlumberger's Paris apartment. The chair is raffia and the wallpanels contain blow-ups of designs for silks.

opposite This period interior espouses a modern style by the inclusion of vivid colours.

suggests, the emotional impact created by juxtaposing many different colours stands outside the sort of control that can normally be exercised over an interior's structure, the shape of its furniture or the location of a fireplace. This makes it the most challenging element in a decorative scheme. Occupants of rooms are constantly changing the colour balance: through their own presence, the arrival of new magazines, the acquisition of an ornament, the placement of a vase of flowers. As the comparison to music also suggests, a rich interplay of many-coloured objects can elicit paradoxical emotions, just as a meaningful melody can

above This collection of brightly coloured gleaming metal and plastic cups creates a vibrant eye-catching kitchen display.

right An ordinary kitchen is enlivened by the random placement of multi-coloured industrial floortiles and the addition of a glass-bead curtain.

produce both tears and elation. Such combinations demand a great deal, both from ourselves and equally from our guests.

Yet there are good reasons to learn to use colour to recognize, express and, ideally, to synthesize emotions. Paul Robertson, leader of the internationally renowned Medici String Quartet since 1971, recently spoke on the universal need to develop richer means of expressing intricacy, inconsistency and emotional insights, now that we are all increasingly interconnected through the technology of information. He said: 'We need more and more complex, subtle and beautiful models of thought and experience with which to cope with this process of change and

relate to it.' He was in this instance, referring directly to music, but as art demonstrates, colour carries its own powerful messages in just the same way.

There are also practical reasons for introducing a range of colours into an interior, particularly high-contrasting colours. These make cupboard doors, stairs, changes in floor level and closely arranged objects easier to distinguish. This has been recognized as important to what is now politely dubbed the 'mature market' (those born prior to 1945), as well as to all people who are partially sighted. Ageing eyes need three times the light that a young person does to see properly, yet they may also be glare-sensitive. Clear, transparent acrylic and glass tabletops, tableware and door-panel inserts are thus hazards for anyone with failing eyesight; a glass tabletop merges with the floorcovering below and, if it also produces a glare, can be blinding.

Day or night, subtle reflections abound – on glass, ceramic, metal or plastic – and produce what the Pre-Raphaelite and Mannerist artists called a lack of pictorial focus. This effect can be found in arrangements as disparate as a clutch of many-coloured contrasting aluminium cups or the nuanced use of colour with light itself, filtered through blistered or leaded coloured glass or tinted muslins and linens hung at the windows. A room carpeted in bright purple will take on that hue in varying degrees of intensity, depending on the nature and angle of the light playing across it; direct bright light reduces the purple's glow, reflected light enhances it. If well chosen, coloured lights further enrich interiors. Using the mood-enhancing qualities of colour, architects and designers such as Philippe Starke and David Gill have devised ways to introduce self-selected hues into interiors – Starke with a rheostat-type switch, Gill with tinted 'jackets' that slide over fluorescent bulbs. Using colour in this way connects us to both later variants of minimalist art, in which the late Dan Flavin was a pioneer in the use of light and colour, and the diverse cultural beliefs in their spirit-restoring qualities.

above Old doors take on a contemporary look when fitted with variously toned glass panes. These eighteenth-century doors are in the home of the French fashion accessory designer, Philippe Model.

complementary colours

Roberto Bergero

The current residence of Parisian decorator Roberto Bergero is a Directoire-style apartment in the Marais, that cosmopolitan area near the Beauborg, known for its narrow streets lined with lively little shops and restaurants but not allowing much light into the residences above them. Without destroying any of the apartment's historical details, this formerly cool, grey neoclassical space soon appeared to be bathed in a warm glow. This transformation into a dramatic, contemporary setting was achieved entirely by Bergero's use of complementary colours.

The creative use of colour is something for which Bergero has achieved international acclaim. The scheme he had chosen for his own home plays upon carefully selected complementary colours – those that sit directly opposite each other on a colour wheel. The principal shades that he has used are just a few degrees off the most contrasting of primary complementaries: red and green. Imagine if, on a clockface, red were at 12, blue at 4, green at 6 and yellow at 8; the rich fuchsia colour, a slightly bluey red, would be at 12.30 and its opposite partner, a yellowish green, at about 6.30. Since warmer tones

right Paint sets the stage in Bergero's living room, not only on the walls, but on the tri-fold firescreen and the rug, of plain sisal carpeting painted with acrylics.

far right Fuchsia and lime are the principal pair of complementary colours used; they are grounded here by the neutral complementaries of white and black.

colour

advance and cooler ones recede, a balance is achieved by using more fuchsia than hot lime. Endless variations of complementary schemes can be developed by using a colour wheel; the lighter the colours, the less dramatic the contrast, but the final effect is always a lively one.

Here Bergero has enriched the main colour palette with a second set of complementary colours, a blue-tinged purple (at 2.30 on our clockface wheel) and its opposite, an orangey yellow/gold. The latter, warm like the lime, is used as a relief to the mainly matt painted surfaces that dominate the interiors. A gold-leaf effect highlights the vase and lamps designed by Bergero and picks out a few carefully selected original details. The gleaming golden tone of the Fornasetti table adds a variation, as do the tangerine satin curtains. The entire colour scheme is grounded and relieved by the use of matt white paint for many of the architectural details and the wooden furniture; the strong verticals thus emphasized increase the illusion of space and height. The addition of black completes Bergero's essay on contrasting colours. Paints supply the majority of the colours. Even the rug in the main reception room has been painted, using acrylics on plain sisal carpeting.

Memory has played a large part in the creation of these interiors. The mixture of tropical-fruit colours evokes Bergero's homeland, Argentina. The land of the tango, itself suggestive of exotic colour combinations, it is also associated with vivid birds and animals, such as the flamingo, whose plumage is brought to mind by the colour of Bergero's apartment. The mouthwatering effect of his combinations might even come from one of Argentina's famous culinary delights, ice cream. Spiritualism and the veneration of the dead are deep-seated in the Argentine culture, so Bergero is not unusual in the homage he pays to his grandmother, whose annual visits from Paris he greatly looked forward to. The beautiful clothes she brought were his first taste of Parisian style. In his present apartment there are strong undertones of the technicolour fashions that restored the fortunes of French couture houses in the 1950s and early 1960s. The chartreuse and shocking pink recall Pierre Balmain evening wear, the touches of black and white Balenciaga and Dior. Bergero acknowledges his mother, who would have worn such gowns, as the source of his passion for decorating. Apparently she had recurrent dreams of curtains, furniture and colours and it was she who gave him his first commission, the redecoration of the family's country home. Bergero's apartment also has distinct undertones of a 1950s Hollywood vision of Paris. Is it real or faux? An apartment or a film set? What is one to make of the pieces, ranging from an eighteenth-century armoire to an Empire-style cardboard table? Bergero's only rule is to banish all that is sad and sombre.

above A headboard painted in tropical colours adds humour, also evoking Bergero's Argentinean homeland.

right The slim vertical lines of gold mouldings and painted edgings on a screen increase the illusion of height in the low-ceilinged dining room.

opposite Here the prominent tones of a Fornasetti 1950s table repeat in the armoire's pleated silk curtains and the black urn and upholstery stripe.

Bergero has reinvented the whimsical, lighthearted combination of modern and antique pieces loved by the *beau monde* and Hollywood alike during the postwar years of his youth. Likewise, reviewing your own childhood memories could inspire the perfect colour scheme. The impetus might be parents, grandparents, favourite films, travels or old decorating books. Take, for example, another complementary colour scheme developed for a friend's dining room, which already had green taffeta curtains. Magenta satin upholstery went on to white-legged deep buttoned chairs, while lettuce-green china and red-handled cutlery was laid on a green-dotted white organdy tablecloth. This combination was based on the mid-century style of the American decorator, Dorothy Draper, whose book, *Decorating is Fun!*, similarly inspired interiors he'd known as a child. If the idea of mixing strong colours is appealing, perusing mid-century fashion magazines, films, decorating books might provide a long-forgotten but loved colour combination just right for your interiors today.

materials

The ingredients for creating an interior have changed tellingly over the past couple of centuries. When Joseph Moxon described the way that early eighteenth-century turners polished their wooden balusters, chair and table legs and ivory handles, he could scarcely have imagined that, some 300 years later, it would be possible to live in a home that contained no wooden furniture, nor that trade in new ivory would be banned in most countries.

Lastly they polish with Bees-wax ... and set a gloss on it with a very dry woollen rag, lightly smeared with salad oil. Ivory they polish with Chalk and water.

Joseph Moxon, **Mechanick Exercises** (1703, new ed. Benno Forman), 1970

However, today's eclecticism ensures that a wide range of materials – both new and old – are important elements of interiors. The key to their use is that each is celebrated for just what it is: oak or polymer, granite or Formica, glass or acrylic, each has its role to play. Their textures and surfaces stimulate the senses, defining the mood of the room.

opposite Varied materials not only offer visual interest; their textures also invite touch and can enhance or muffle sound.

materials matter

above and right Natural materials will always provide subtle variations in shading and texture within the interior. The individual beauty of such features is highlighted in these three limewashed wooden cabinets and the enchanting detail of a bowl made entirely from quills by Dai Rees, both results of the fusion of natural materials and acquired human artistry.

Materials define the texture of an interior. If we include the food and flowers that complete our lives, they stimulate all our senses. We know our surfaces through touch; we hear the difference between metal and glass, wool and wood; we smell polishes and scented candles as well as flowers. The act of engaging with a room is far more than just looking, it is an all-encompassing experience.

Texture is a matter of degree and scale; minute differences affect our senses. Because we are so attuned to texture, we use it as an analogy for abstract concepts of quality, character and structure. We appreciate the rich texture of life. In wine tasting, when discussing the small variations of taste and richness, we speak of its texture. More generally our understanding of the behaviour and qualities of materials often underpins our shorthand terms for human characteristics. Wooden suggests both dry and rigid, transparent both free from pretence and easily seen through. Even plastic has entered our language, as a term for people who are both artificial and gullible, capable of being moulded. As these examples indicate, material-based descriptions are often used to explain our exclusion of particular people from our small world. When we attach to people labels that describe their superficial outer self in this way, we imply a preference for multi-faceted and well-balanced characters, ones that we can explore and be comfortable with. We seek just the same in interiors. A variety of materials and textures in our surroundings is a basic human need, and its absence is part of the disturbing effect of an all-white room or a snow or sand storm where there are no points of comfort or reassurance.

Nature in its overwhelming and inspiring variety provides unlimited examples of textures. Sensuous appreciation of its range of landscapes and plant and animal life is one of the main reasons why time in the mountains, country or seaside is still valued by urban dwellers everywhere. Because of this, love of natural materials runs deep in our consciousness. In the past these materials were often the principal character-building elements of buildings, inside and out. Brick, wood, plaster, cement, clay, adobe and stone, in all their varying tones and textures, have been the basis for our slowly evolving relationship with the built environment. Today their exposed use for indoor walls and features inevitably suggests a rustic or timeless setting. So, too, do stone, terracotta and wooden floors, all so fundamental to interiors that they are able to support both modern and traditional decorative schemes. Plastered walls are particularly neutral, no doubt because of the universality of clay, the basis of plaster's most ancient and widely used form, which we still recognize today in adobe. Nevertheless, because many of these staples retain an association with the region in which they were originally found, cultural resonances come unbidden with their selection. Materials such as Portland stone, London brick and Western red cedar even display their origins in their name.

above The rugged surface of pine cladding will add a rustic touch to any interior. This is accentuated here by the many shades of natural and brown – from fur drapes to furniture upholstery and carpeting.

From plants we have garnered an equally wide range of ingredients for the construction of fittings and furniture. From materials such as wicker, rattan, bamboo, raffia, straw, jute and hemp come a vast array of products, including lightweight furniture, boxes, blinds, screens and paper. Flax and cotton, together with the animal fibres silk and wool, still give us a huge choice of textiles. They also define for us – through their surfaces – what soft, silky, velvety, woolly, crisp and diaphanous mean, characteristics so sought after by humans that the replication of these has driven forward the refinement of manmade and synthetic fibres. Texture is a fundamental part of fabric's makeup and function, and our first and most intense experience of it.

Of all manmade things, textiles are the only category with which we are nearly constantly and intimately surrounded, literally, from cradle to grave. So it is through textiles and their functionally related allies – furs and leather – that interiors are related to fashion. Today the links between these two fields are instantaneous. For example, induced by concerns for animal welfare, the development of 'fun furs' made an evident impact on the winter 1999/2000 fashions. By February *House Beautiful* was cajoling its readers: 'You're wearing red pony-skin mules and carrying a leopard-print handbag. Why not dress your home up in the same sort of hip animal-pelt accessories?' Since fashion has also propelled a renewed appreciation for hand-stitched and dyed fabrics from the Far East and India, these, too, are readily available for use in interiors. Amid all this, futuristic developments have not been set aside; laser-printed and patinated fabrics, new methods of

above Decorative windows can be custom-made, as here, or ingeniously created by varnishing printed images on to the glass.

right Below a French mid-twentieth-century tapestry, planks adorned with bags and other personal items bestow an individual touch.

opposite The inviting textures of a wallhung Susani and other old textiles turn a sofa into a cosy retreat.

permanent embossing and pleating, heat-and colour-conducting fibres, and microfine spinning offer endless new possibilities. Among twentieth-century manmade materials, those that can be moulded or shaped into different forms under pressure and/or heat are called plastic, a general name for a host of substances with the property: acrylic, casein, celluoid, Bakelite, PVC, and so on. Their invention derived from experience with natural plastics, such as gutta percha, used in Europe during the mid-nineteenth century for a host of things (most notably ear trumpets), and semi-synthetics, such as vulcanite from rubber, which in the same period was made into items including boxes and pens.

Every material we use in our homes is a vivid example of human ingenuity. Most have a long history within interiors. Glass, pottery, metalwork, marble, textiles, leather, wood and paper were already highly developed 2,000 years ago and, in forms that we would recognize today, were integrated into interiors by the sixteenth century. By then there were also many supplementary

decorative treatments such as stamping and embossing of leather wallcoverings and their replacement, wallpaper. The beginnings of world trade increased the understanding and supply of colourants – metal oxides for enamelling, glass and ceramics; pigments for oil paintings, watercolours and paper; and dyes for textiles and leather. The nineteenth-century explosion of machine patterning, material innovations and synthetic-colouring processes made decoration with *objets d'art,* a middle-class phenomenon that retained an appreciation for traditional materials and skills.

Traditional materials and skills remain alive to this day. In fact the current interest in metalwork, especially wrought iron, has revived the fortunes of creative blacksmiths. The greater concern for global communities means that – taking just clay, for example – we can readily find handthrown vases, tableware and cookware from around the world, and Indian and African textiles still patterned with an overdyed mud resist; selfbuild specialists can advise on or supply adobe bricks. Add to these the mass-produced items such as tiles, and you could easily create a room of one material, although it would probably prove too sterile for our materials-hungry nature. This explains why those 'all-white' rooms were not really all white, but enriched and enlivened with shaggy, rough and deeply articulated surfaces.

The distinctions our fingers can make between one surface and another are enhanced by what we hear. The ping of crystal establishes its quality; the thud of earthenware distinguishes it from porcelain; our footfall tells us without looking whether the tiles beneath us are terracotta or linoleum. The clinking of glasses is symbolic of welcome, thanks and celebration. The clang and clatter of metal pots and kitchen utensils are part of many people's fond memories of a warm and welcoming childhood home. Sounds are everywhere. The swish and rustle of curtains or the sigh of a well-stuffed old leather chair when we sit on it are essential parts of what makes an interior feel comfortable. As these examples illustrate, softer and more pliable materials tend to muffle sound, while harder materials amplify it. Madrid, said to be the noisiest city on earth to live in, is partly made so by the extensive use of tiling over walls and floors. Choosing materials with this in mind means considering ambient sound levels and how peaceful or lively you want your home to be.

Colour can also muffle texture. Highly contrasting hues detract from textural variety, by attracting the eye to patterns and forms and away from small details. Closely ranged, nuanced tones, whether dark or light, allow diverse surfaces to come to the forefront of our attention. Since colour speaks to our emotions and textures appeal to our physical responses, an intense combination of many kinds of both results in a room that is far from restful. The effect is rather like trying to talk and listen at the same time. Concentrating on doing one or the other, as we know from experience, is the only way to communicate and, as in life, so in interiors.

above The juxtaposition of soft and hard surfaces enhances subtle colours and textures; here added richness comes from the shadows playing over these Moroccan tea glasses.

left Multi-faceted beads draw attention to their surface; strung as a curtain, they increase the sense of space in the room beyond and chime softly when moved.

far left The sleek, bright surfaces of a tightly grouped collection of handpainted ceramics attract the eye from across the room.

interior accessories

The interplay among materials is as important as the relationship between colour and materials. As with all things, too much variety can be overpowering. Satisfying arrangements of objects share something in common, so that the subtle distinctions between them are highlighted, rather than overlooked.

Looking at materials is part of what makes objects of interest to us; through our eyes we recognize and appreciate their form and surface qualities, and the way together they create a visual whole. The assembling of various elements into groups is directly related to collage and, as in art, it is both a creative exercise in its own right and a means of exploring visual effects before committing to a finished composition. Many of us make collages unconsciously. A noticeboard, a refrigerator door, a basket into which odds and ends are temporarily dropped, a coat rack, a

right Highly textured and brightly coloured treasures can hold their own against each other.

opposite Reflections glinting off shiny objects are enriched by grouping them together in front of a mirror or on a glass-topped surface.

below Interiors are like a collage, open to constant revision and exploration; this collage of natural-toned finds is pulled together by the neutral shade of the wall.

kitchen shelf – the list can be as varied as our daily lives. Certain activities even invite collaging. Bathing and cooking, for example, are made easier by having everything needed to hand. In the process, hanging devices, open shelves and nearby counters become props in the constantly changing vignettes we create every day. In this way we build up a vast, intuitive knowledge of the way objects visually interact with each other and the way changes in daylight and artificial light can transform what we see.

Light plays on every surface in a different way. Smooth, hard materials, such as silver, glass and porcelain, glint in a way readily distinguishable from the gleam of the slightly more textured surfaces of pewter, acrylic and earthenware. The sheen of silk, produced by the fineness and length of its filaments, is distinguishable from the glow of chintzed cotton, made so by glazing or pressing flat. These characteristics are easily spotted, even from the opposite side of a room. They also attract the eye. Matt surfaces, on the other hand, tend to recede, and therefore can act as an effective foil for the glistening objects set on them; this is why jewellers so often line their cases with black velvet, which combines in one cloth the most light-absorbing of colours

and textures. The reverse is also true: shells, fossils, stones and anything else with a rugged texture can hold their own against shiny surfaces and are often found grouped on tiled surfaces, highly polished wood or in front of a mirror. It follows that to make the background part of the arrangement, all need to be similarly textured.

Textural qualities within the interior are enhanced when light is raking, that is, coming in from one side rather than flat on. Raking light highlights the ridges of a surface, and throws the furrows into deep shadow. In nature we see this effect every time the sun is low on the horizon. In contrast to reflected light, which produces a soft, dispersed illumination, raking light makes

calm concentration, such as kitchens and studies, and is better reserved for areas where we have the time to fully appreciate the effect that it creates.

Of the many ways in which we can introduce visual entertainment to an interior, *trompe l'oeil* is the best known. This artistic technique literally fools the eye by rendering a surface three-dimensional, complete with shadows, perspective and the odd 'flaw' or two. The dramatic effect of shadows need not be restricted to faux effects. Anything with bold, vigorous texture or sculptural form can be lit to emphasize its planes and movement, whether they are jagged or organic. The drama of a formally dressed table, covered with tureens, platters, glasses and other essentials of varying heights and shapes is best achieved with candelabra, the flickering flame of the candles providing both form-enhancing shadows and light that itself is in motion.

Different materials grouped according to shared forms can also make interesting juxtapositions. This generally finds expression in displays of groups of plates on a dresser; similarly framed engravings, drawings or photographs, trinketboxes and pillboxes and any number of things whose form is part of their function. But combinations emphasizing form alone can be found, too. Rounded, sphere-like shapes are a good example. Balls, globes, eggs, early lightbulbs and stones share sculptural similarities. On the whole, though, it is the marriage of material, form and function that most pleases us. The result of our appreciation of our planet's geology and plant life and animal life, it is expressed in gatherings of stones, shells or leaves, functional elements of nature that we find beautiful. Just as the spiralling undulations or splaying ridges of a shell, providing strength to protect the creature within, are appreciated best when the shell is intact, well-designed objects have a similar cohesion, allowing the material to do what it does best.

Plastic objects that have successfully found their form and function have been with us for long enough to be familiar things.

top A collection of stainless-steel kitchen implements hung from chains reinforce the metallic theme of this kitchen and provide a useful storage strategy.

above This *trompe l'oeil* wallpaper with frames placed over it demonstrates how shadows – real or fake – give prominence to surface textures and forms.

the surfaces it crosses appear livelier, even bristling with energy. In consequence it is seldom appropriate for use in spaces that are designed for

By 1907, when the synthetic plastic Bakelite was patented, it was already clear that the forms best suited to these materials were unadorned and organic. Today the same principles of plasticity give rise to a wide range of objects, from sculptural, moulded polyester-resin furniture to acrylic vases and light fittings. Some have even changed our ideas about how certain things should look. Prime examples are the plastics made from glass fibre bound together with polyester or epoxy resins, in use since the late 1940s. Used within a few years by Charles Eames, Eero Saarinen and others for chairs in which sculptural form was explored, these challenged the line between art and design, which still remains hazy. Lightweight plastic containers are so easy to glue together or cut down that they also have creative potential, for example, in the use of making unique recycled objects (as illustrated above).

above Ranging from tribal to post-modern, such unusual combinations are linked through their detailed surfaces and the texture of rugs and cloths playing against the plastic shapes of the 'homemade' standing lamp.

The judgements we use as we bring together materials are personal. It may be form rather than surface that appeals; by arranging and rearranging we can observe the changing emphasis and discover our preferences. We need never arrive at a final, 'fixed' arrangement, to be displayed frozen and suspended in time as if in a gallery. This is because, as closely entwined as art and interiors are, what we express of ourselves in our homes is constantly evolving.

food and flowers

above A pewter vase forms the basis of a suitably simple but elegant display of leaves and vegetables, by Sophie Conran.

opposite Open storage makes for an informal kitchen, the ingredients here drawn together by the strong colour contrasts and geometric patterns.

Many of the most publicized minimalist interiors of the 1990s were the coffee bars, restaurants and hotels designed with the 'business-buzz' generation in mind. These are the sleekest of spaces, whether an amalgam of natural woods and metals, or Formica from top to toe. The food, it seemed, was equally minimalist: espresso and sushi reigned supreme. But the photographs that recorded and promoted such interiors seldom captured the reality. The truth was that it was the laden table that appealed, even for the most aspiring minimalist restaurateur or host – the flowers, the chopsticks or cutlery, the napkins and the different dishes, each a carefully considered concoction, with its special complexity of texture and colour to beguile the diners' senses.

The company we share our food with matters, too. At home this has been reflected in our kitchen, the most informal and intimate of reception rooms. The process of preparing food, cooking, washing and packing away, as well as the sharing of meals with friends and family, gives the kitchen a comforting, welcoming quality. Increasingly they have became informal, cosy places. Fitted kitchens came to seem unfit as backdrops for the entertaining of guests; Welsh dressers, handpainted cabinets and rustic touches were much more welcoming. For the stay-at-homes (a separate species from the couch potato) cooking has become a serious matter, and having all the implements to hand is not only expedient but proven to be attractive. For travellers there has been the delight of another country's way with food, the tapas bar becoming a much-copied concept. Margaret Visser, a Canadian writer, argues that food is so vital to us that we

David – declared that the kitchen was king. Discussing the 'sociable kitchen' he observed that as the century's end approached, the living room was 'shrinking (metaphorically), the media room lights up few pixels, the mud room creates an imagined sense of cleanliness and order. But the kitchen is on the rampage ... Almost all the downstairs uses of the house are now expected to be accommodated at least partially in the kitchen in an open plan style that encompasses entertaining, eating and cooking, and might also accommodate a desk with space for a computer and telephone, a television, a relaxing space including a sofa, a children's play area with some storage ...' He might well have also added space to display collections of cooking utensils, tableware and practical and decorative *objets trouvés*.

The significance of preparing and serving food – and arranging flowers, too – lies not only in satisfying the basic need to eat or entertain. It offers us a constant encounter with the design process. Since we undertake these activities frequently and often unthinkingly, what we choose to do with food and flowers is often a good indication of what we would really like to be doing with our interiors. The way our crockery and staples are arranged in the cupboards can be equally revealing. Conversely, in cooking and serving meals, as well as in displaying dried or fresh flowers and greenery, we can consciously experiment with unusual combinations of ingredients, playing with contrasting colours and materials, or developing interest through the juxtaposition of different textures. Scale can be explored too; think how unappetizing meals would be if everything were the same size and shape. Through food and flowers, we can investigate the effects of virtually every combination of colours, textures and forms each day, especially if we also play with table settings, so temporary an arrangement that they invite risk taking.

Adding what is today available from the numerous retail sources to what already lies in our cupboards, there are endless possibilities. Under the influence of Oriental serving traditions

underestimate the information it contains about our tastes, quite literally, and about the times we live in. The concept of 'a little of this, a little of that' seems to sum up the trends today.

In the midst of the 1990s' boom in preprepared foods, kitchens actually became more rather than less significant, by providing a secure psychological hub for time-pressed working partners, two-income families and single loft-dwellers alike. Towards the end of 1996 Johnny Grey – the renowned American kitchen designer and nephew of the legendary cook Elizabeth

Western tableware manufacturers now offer a greatly expanded variety of serving platters, plates and bowls that are designed to stack one on top of the other. They need not match; it might instead be a colour or theme that binds them together. The theme could be easy to spot, as in the case of pictorial tableware, or clear only to those who know you well. My own array of plates, for example, are patterned with checked rims, all over plaids and the like, and together delight me because these are all also weave patterns. As in this case, some could be old and some new. The permutations of such products are limitless and can be altered with ease from subtle to strident. Such responsiveness to mood is a fundamental part of our ever-changing relationship with food, and it contributes equally to our response to both public and private entertaining.

The lessons we learn through the activities of preparing food, arranging flowers and plants and dressing a table for dinner can easily be transferred to other aspects of interiors. Groupings of cushions, ornaments, pictures and furniture can be seen as offering a similar interplay of ingredients. Both food and floral displays are, first of all, contained. The plate, bowl, vase or tub acts as an anchoring device, defining the parameters of our experimentations; a table does the same thing for a mealtime arrangement. An area of strong colour, a large picture or mirror, a dominant piece of furniture, a mantelpiece, a change in floor treatment, all offer the same anchor to groups of objects.

In addition, and as we know from looking so often at different foods on a plate or many stems in a vase, we actually perceive tightly grouped objects as one thing. A bookcase with its many coloured spines becomes a patterned grid; similar objects hung shoulder to shoulder over an expanse of wall become a single essay on a theme, and a focal point of attention. Because of the attention-grabbing qualities of interesting groupings such as these, we are also better able to appreciate the variety represented within, and that is why the close arrangement of

objects can actually highlight their individual differences, rather than detracting from

above Tightly grouping objects highlights their differences in scale, outline and detail; such close arrangements also make a single visual statement, especially suitable for unusual things.

them. In contrast, evenly-distancing objects of similar size tends to make comparisons more difficult. This display approach also conveys formality, placing the emphasis on the things themselves rather than the setting, which is why public galleries and museums present certain types of art in this way. Groupings are much more intimate and, as we recognize with food that is made more appetizing by its arrangement, the end result is in consequence likely to be more inviting.

unexpected elements

There is a fascination with the hybrid among present-day artists, designers and makers that results in a marriage of the ordinary with the unexpected. While seemingly unusual, in fact as an approach it has a long history. While we might not wish to go as far as to emulate the seventeenth-century Capuchin cemetery in Rome, where human bones were used to create delicate and elaborate wall decorations, there are countless unusual materials available to enhance interiors, and an equal abundance of quirky concepts that can provide inspiration.

Inventive though our distant ancestors may have been, the current prevalence of experimentation in interiors owes most to the foundations laid down by Surrealist artists in the earlier twentieth century. The wit and irreverence suggested by bringing unexpected elements into a room is indebted to Surrealism through that movement's focus on spontaneous techniques such as collage and frottage (rubbings taken from everyday things). The artists' aim was to use impromptu combinations of unrelated things to resolve the conflict between dreams and reality. Melding aspiration with fact is the very stuff of interiors. It is little wonder that, at a time when the world seems especially contradictory, there is an evident relish for *trompe l'oeil* effects, for the oversized and for the incongruous, all surreal in their impact.

Creative activities evolve slowly, firstly beginning with experiments by a handful and gradually spiralling outwards in ever-greater circles. In these terms 70-odd years was not a

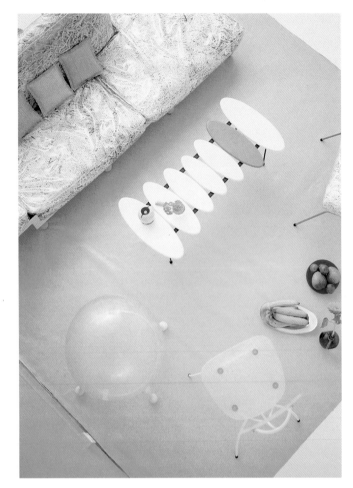

below A collection of old pennies garnish the lid of a wooden toilet seat, proving that even the simplest of household objects can be treated in a decorative and eye-catching way.

long time to wait to arrive at the present situation, in which significant numbers of interiors incorporate unexpected elements. Because we still live in a period in which there is a great focus on new materials and their behavioural and sculptural qualities, these are the prime motivators behind the diverse range of imaginative approaches to interiors and their contents. In comparison, surface treatments themselves – that is repeat patterns – take a backseat, content to provide an eclectic selection of ethnic, retro and historical motifs, or a rich texture. This said, the exception is in the matter of scale; the majority of innovative textiles and wallpapers, and other wall treatments, too, are bold in size and conception. The imagery may well be historical but, rendered large, the impact is thoroughly modern. As a further indication of the melding of art and design, the source might equally be a Renaissance painting or a technical drawing. Laser and other new printing processes are already lifting former restrictions on the fineness of detail and size of repeat; the same processes as these also support tailor-made wallcoverings, supplied by specialists or homemade by the adventurous.

Homemade details offer the widest scope for invention. There are age-old techniques that can be adapted to today's use: decoupage, papier mâché, origami and the many twisting, binding and braiding processes. Even macramé (the relatively simple knotting technique that everyone who lived through the seventies tries to forget) is ripe for a reassessment on a larger scale, and with different materials. All manner of things can be made with these simple skills. For furniture take a lead from the Brazilian Campana brothers, who designed the Zig-Zag stool for Edra, using only a simple metal hoop with legs, intertwined with coloured plastic cord. Or from Darcy Turner, an artist in residence at a London school, who rolls old newspapers into loose tubes, brushes them with wallpaper paste and compresses them into rods, which are bound with cable ties to make chairs, stools and tables. Cardboard offers possibilities, too. Tubes are strong and can be lashed together for a

above left Unexpected materials are the stuff of New York designer Gaston Marticorena's furniture; here a sofa has transparent plastic cushion covers stuffed with wood shavings and shredded newspaper.

right Blown-up laser copies of Mannerist cherubs make a rich and intriguing wall covering.

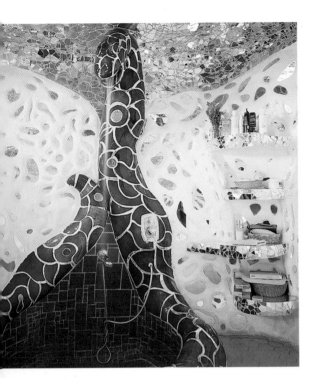

above Inspired by Gaudi, Niki de Saint Phalle's Tuscan sculpture garden can be seen by appointment; one sculpture harbours a 'sea-monster' shower, adorned with broken and randomly cut tiles.

screen, a solid table or, depending on their diameter, storage for items large and small. Often the best place to look for inspiration is in the garage, loft or least-used cupboard or drawer. Inevitably there is something there to spark off an idea. The rewards are twofold: more storage space and good use of something lying idle.

As with all things, these unexpected elements need to be used judiciously. And it is wise to begin with something small if the technique is newly acquired. Even straightforward processes can be time consuming. The wallpapers decorated by Tracy Kendall in her London studio illustrate that the deceptively simple may not be; dotted with sequins, buttons, beads and baubles, Kendall attaches these by handsewing, and it takes an entire day to embellish one metre. Far better, especially if time is at a premium, to think creatively about ready-made things, even standard decorating items. Carpet tape, floortiles, walltiles and mirrors, for example, come in a vast array of sizes, shapes and finishes. Aside from using these in unexpected combinations and places, tiled and mirrored surfaces can be interspersed with some that are the wrong way around, their rough side up. Beyond this, there are all the fashion items that are worthy of display. The precedent for this has already been set. It used to be common to see bronzed baby shoes in American homes and, given the sculptural finesse of many finely made shoes – and hats and bags for that matter – there is every reason to bring them out from

hiding. Take the Surrealist's subversive lead. This was laid out within the first *Surrealist Manifesto* by André Breton and stressed the 'higher reality of certain neglected forms'.

Hardware, boating and industrial-product suppliers also provide a wealth of possibilities among their offerings. In *Rethink* Tom Dixon presents a useful range of sources and ideas; he also argues eloquently for the need to look again at the 'invisible' objects all around us, anonymously designed and capable of being subverted for uses other than those intended. As he admits, this is not a new idea. 'Almost anybody might use an oil drum as a barbecue, and all over the world plastic carrier bags become rubbish bins. It is universally accepted in junior circles that a car inner tube makes the perfect toy boat... The hub of a wheel is variously used as an anvil or a table base according to need. And it was not surprising to find that in the orbiting space station MIR, cosmonauts used wire coat hangers as radio aerials.' However, there is something new in the motivation behind the current rethinking: now self-expression as much as necessity is the mother of these inventions.

Designers themselves are, of course, equally likely these days to be using that human knack of rethinking. Old detergent bottles have become a kind of plastic chipboard in the hands of London-based Jane Atfield, who also makes chairs from stacks of industrial felt, Geisha screens from faulty yard-rulers, and childproof seating from straw bails wrapped in tarpaulins.

In America, Karyl Sisson handbuilds exquisite bowls and containers from tape measures. The Italian Jacopo Fogginis has achieved a

above A hanging forest of Jacopo Fogginis lamps adds both colour and sculptural impact to his Milan apartment.

left Carpet tape in many colours and widths literally binds together the walls and floors of this eccentric interior.

worldwide reputation for his lamps formed out of methacrylate, a synthetic material used mainly in car reflectors, foglights, smoglights and the flashing lights of police cars. It seems perfectly apt that Fogginis' inspiration was the Surrealist Salvador Dali. To adventure into the realm of the unexpected materials yourself requires no training, but simply an open mind and sense of fun.

wonderful wood

Philip Agee

Philip Agee is an accidental craftsman, a painter and printmaker turned cabinetmaker. His basic love is wood, and it shows in Muleland, his San Francisco home/office/studio, and in the chairs, cabinets and other things he makes for his clients.

Muleland demonstrates the diverse ways in which wood can enliven an interior. Agee extols its many advantages. To start with, it is 'accessible; it feels good; it smells good – some oaks smell like celery, while walnuts are bitter.' It requires very little upkeep. Except for wiping up spills, it needs no spray polishing, which only dims the natural gleam of varnished wood. As Agee puts it, 'it is very simple; even a wooden dining table used daily need only be waxed twice a year.' It can also be used in many ways, as evidenced by the humble material plywood. Many of the sculptural shapes of the mid-twentieth-century designer chairs, and those by Agee, result from bending plywood. In Agee's kitchen, a thin-plied birch – called airplane ply after its original function – has been used to make rounded cabinet doors. As used on Muleland's kitchen floor, plywood underlay offers inspiration for us all. Intending eventually

right The painted plywood underlay on Muleland's kitchen floor has become visually richer through wear.

above far right Wood is a perfect foil for other materials, and when waxed its softly gleaming surface brings warmth to any interior; here bands of different-coloured woods add subtle detail.

to cover it, as is usual, with tiles or linoleum, Agee temporarily painted it. Then he overpainted it with big multi-coloured squares. As the well-walked areas became worn, the effect became richer. Plywood underlay is easy and inexpensive to obtain and install, or have installed over old wooden floors, and it need not be limited to kitchens. Painted, it is ideal as a quick, temporary solution, as a means of testing out a colour scheme to be made permanent later in an overlay, or simply as a way of creating a distinctive floor covering. It can also be buffed and varnished, to let its natural grain and colour provide a soft-toned background for rugs or furniture.

As the Muleland interiors demonstrate, choosing wood does not limit the colours in a room. Wood can be stained. Agee cites the small red things he has made from oak, its grain open enough to absorb the colourant easily and yet remain visible. In its natural tones the visual warmth of wood is also a perfect foil for other materials, whether glass, metal, plastics or even concrete, a slab of which Agee has incorporated into his drawingboard as a particularly hardwearing work-surface. He also points out that a room need not contain only the same woods. Mixing their nuances of browns, blacks and warm neutrals puts the focus on

the different grains' subtle textural qualities, a point emphasized by his reference grid of small hardwood squares, arranged alphabetically from alder and ash through cherry and holly and on to redwood and walnut. Even their names evoke a medley of colour, texture and scents.

Agee established his business just seven years ago, but has been making furniture for some 25 years. He began by making pieces for himself and restoring furniture for others. This, he says, was how he learnt his craft, urged on by the fact that 'it was fun to see how a drawer could be put together and the many ways these might be hung.' When something especially tricky came up, he sought advice from a specialist restorer, associated with a mid-twentieth-century furniture gallery frequented by Agee and his partner, Stephen Penkowsky, an exhibition designer who shares Agee's appreciation of period design. Restoring simple wooden furniture and objects takes patience but is rewarding. Wood is a forgiving material and, provided the surface is not of veneer or marquetry, can tolerate less than perfect stripping, sanding and

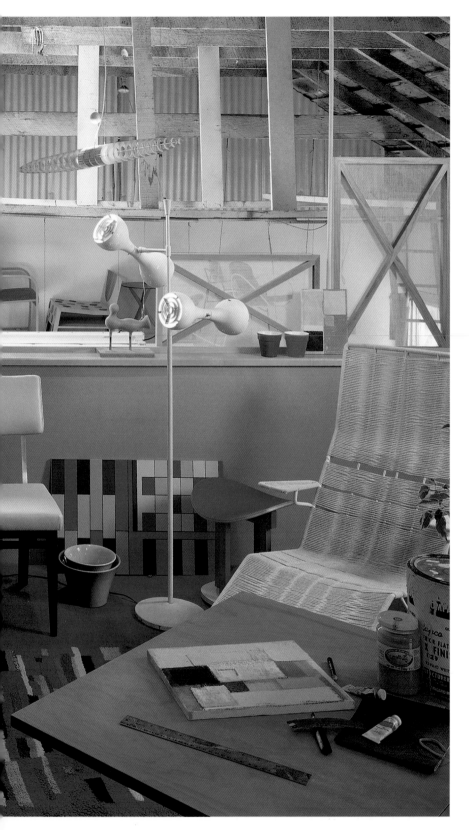

refinishing; in old pieces the cracks, dents and scratches can be part of its character. For more complicated projects, it is wise to follow Agee's example and find a 'tame guru' to advise. Precious pieces, whether their value is sentimental or monetary, should be entrusted to an established expert.

Traditional skills and materials are still widely available today. It is well worth considering commissioning handmade furniture, or one special piece. There are several good reasons for doing so. You can ensure that the woods selected are not endangered but farmed, as are the American native hardwoods that Agee uses. There is a chance it will become a family heirloom, and meanwhile your involvement in the process will ensure that the piece fits your character. This means that such pieces can move anywhere with you. For example, Agee feared problems with the things he had made for a client who later moved, but everything worked. A bedroom cabinet is now in the living room; what remains unchanged is the client's relationship with the piece. In addition, Agee's pieces are finished on all sides, so they can be used free standing or perpendicular to a wall, instead of having to be flat against one. Whether choosing from among inherited, found, or commissioned objects and furniture, this is a feature to look for. Try, also, to be what Agee describes as the perfect buyer: 'have ideas, express what you want and react to the design, even if only to say that bad personal associations means anything but oak will do.' In this way, you become part of the design process, making the resulting piece more uniquely yours than mere ownership provides.

above far left and left Both the office and living spaces at Muleland prove that a room need not be decorated all in the same wood. On display in the latter is Agee's collection of miniature chairs positioned to show their sculptural qualities, including on the right a DCW (Dining Chair Wood), designed by Charles Eames in the 1950s.

looking back

The marketing of the past, from the 1950s to the 1750s and even earlier, made headlines in the 1980s and 1990s, as merchandisers cashed in on a growth 'industry'. Undoubtedly it helped that throughout the 1980s the English country-house look prevailed. By the 1990s that style had, for many, lost its bloom. Nevertheless, as a legacy it left behind a taste for the mixture of pieces from different periods, emitting that subtle suggestion of generations of acquisitions, handed down over the centuries.

... heritage design, together with our heritage, is here to stay.

Giles Verlade, heritage consultant
'Time will Tell', **Design Week**, November 1990

Whether the style gurus liked it or not, nostalgic packaging of everything from soaps to soups boosted sales. Emboldened by the surfeit of choice and aided by a new 'take' on traditional interiors, themselves explored in many different ways by designers and shown with diverse emphases in magazine features, home-owners in recent years have not been shy to go on mixing and matching, often with surprising results.

opposite Ordinary things from the not-so-distant past – here the 1950s – bring a touch of pleasing familiarity to any interior.

packaged in the past

The past is a complex and abstract notion. One of the clearest indications of this is to be found in interiors. There we might well express both our own unique past and the more generalized past – bounded by region, nation, race or religion. But we can live in equal comfort with elements that derive mainly from other people's pasts. The latter are typically romantic or idealized pasts, constantly redefined and absorbed anew. In interiors the influence of the past can be found running in tandem with up-to-date styles as far back, at least, as the sixteenth century; it is also subject to the same impulses that form current taste.

The new use of past styles seems to rest on two factors. One is anonymity; furniture types or interior treatments from the past that become 'classics' are, as a result, the easiest to make our own. Persian and tribal rugs, new or old, typify this 'neutral' kind of past, adding a touch of luxury or timelessness to an interior without laying claim to any other aspect of the culture that created them. The richly textured and coloured interiors of fortresses, abbeys, chateaux and castles appeal to us in a similar way; the power and authority they once represented has been transmuted over centuries into the less domineering attributes of stability and longevity. That so many aspects of non-Western and Pre-Renaissance histories are part of current interiors is explained by the other factor at work, an element that makes them timely – a parallel attitude shared by underlying trends then and now.

For all its eccentricity, the prevailing attitude projected now by fashionable interiors is stability. But how can this be so? After all, the overriding vision is currently, at its most extreme, an amalgam of glamour and decay, or, at its least, stylishness combined with casual disarray. The first clue to the desire for something less hasty is the prevalence of revived twentieth-century styles – Art Deco, architect-designed furniture of the 1930s to the 1960s, hippy ethnicity of the 1970s and so on – whether knowingly selected or unconsciously incorporated. Stepping into a new century, we seem unprepared to sever ourselves from the

one in which we were born. The second, related clue is that we also seem to be settling down. Baby Boomers, everyone born between 1945 and 1964, have moved more times than any other generation to date but, according to the USA's National Association of the Remodeling Industry's 1999 forecast, have grown accustomed to their neighborhoods and would rather remodel their current residence to suit their personalities and characters than pack up and move to another location. A strong economic force, Boomers influence trends in virtually every industry; they are responsible for the recent dramatic growth in gallery and auction-house sales of mid-twentieth-century furniture. The so-called Generation X, those born between 1965 and 1980, lack the money and credit of Baby Boomers; as a result, in the USA this generation has rediscovered and remodelled the smaller and earlier twentieth-century houses and apartments, often seeking appropriate furnishings in the process. To a lesser degree (because more older housing stock exists in Europe, for example), the same trend has occurred elsewhere. Overall the result is a willingness of designers, manufacturers, auctioneers and dealers worldwide to supply furnishings and memorabilia in a wide range of twentieth-century styles, turning many pieces of furniture – even ones hardly 40 years old – into classics.

above This Loire valley interior, decorated by Jacques Grange, displays an artful clutter that achieves unity through the combination of rustic wooden furniture from several periods and the 'neutral' classics, such as the coir floorcovering, linen panel-curtains and simple shelving.

far left A classic 1940s leather chair exudes serene comfort, whether it is set within a sombre period style or a more contemporary decor.

that if the look you are after is one of permanence and social consciousness, it is to be found by including broad swathes of colour and a judiciously placed, traditionally patterned rug.

The theatrical drama that can be found in many interiors today can also be linked to the lingering glance at the twentieth century. Whatever historical period individual pieces or entire rooms suggest, there is little doubt that they frequently draw upon the most widely shared vision of the past, as represented on film. Hollywood, from its outset cosmopolitan in its sources and the designers it employed, provided us with a chronicle of evolving modern and period tastes for most of the past century. It even created its own style. 'Hollywood baroque'

above Gilded furniture, azure-blue walls and dramatic lighting give this interior a 'Hollywood baroque' air.

far right As shown by this Lutyens' 1903 redecoration of Lindesfarne Castle, Holy Island, woods, rough-hewn walls and brass candlesticks, formally arranged, convey permanence and understated luxury.

Further clues to the desire for stability are the interior elements that suggest stronger interests in home, family and the environment. If we look into the past for instances when humanitarian issues were high on the agenda, the Renaissance and the Arts and Crafts Movement are prime examples. They, too, came to place Persian, Turkish or similarly styled rugs in rooms containing richly coloured or textured surfaces. It is interesting that this should be so, for Arts and Crafts designers, among whom William Morris is the best known, were themselves generally looking back for inspiration to pre-Renaissance periods. Nevertheless, they ended up adapting elements key to Renaissance interiors, which were similarly influenced by earlier classical periods and the immediate past. In the sixteenth and late nineteenth centuries, these features were used in different ways (on tables during the earlier period) and our use of them is different again. Yet all the evidence suggests

was the decadent partner of 1930s streamlined *moderne*. It drew on the one hand from Iberian tastes – rough plaster walls, wrought iron fittings, richly toned soft furnishings – and, on the other, brought in curvaceous forms, gilding, chandeliers and mirrors from French and Italian baroque. Surrealist touches were also thrown in, particularly apt given that these were often expressed through the shadows and emphasis of shapes provided by well-judged lighting. In its present-day incarnation it is only for the strong-hearted.

Incorporating the past into the present demands an eye alert to the themes that different periods share with our own. For example, for those present-day wants – a combination of theatricality, vibrant colours, middle-class values, comfort, mass-production, and elegance of design – we could have turned for inspiration to the Biedermeier style, developed in the Austrian Empire and the Germanic States between about 1810 and 1830. It had already experienced a revival in that brief 'bright' period around 1989–93. However, in its pure form it represents the stolid merchant, Herr Biedermeier (which roughly translates into 'plain Smith'), whose materialistic concerns distracted him from larger issues. Many of the styles of the 1920s and 1930s that are in vogue now are indebted to the Biedermeier style, but – crucially – Art Deco and other interwar movements were also inspired by African and Oceanic arts, which makes these far more relevant to life in integrated and ethnically diverse communities today. A similar mixture of tribal and western inspirations can be found in the Contemporary style that swept in during the 1950s, and on, really, until the English country-house look took hold in the 1980s. Despite their often strikingly different details, it is this global outlook that runs as a constant through the 1920s to the 1970s, and this may well account for the way in which certain objects from these decades sit so well together. The widely admired work of Jacques Grange, a French designer closely associated with this blend, indicates how effective this package can be, and underscores our renewed interest in ideas and trends that also characterized the 'long' mid-twentieth century. The contribution of the past to today's interiors is ever present and continually surrounds us. It may be expressed by the inclusion of the things from a particular period, by the suggestion of a retrospective mood through the choice of colours and lighting, or simply by the formal arrangement of objects in a room. What ever the case, the goal is an ambience rather than perfect authenticity or loyalty to a historical era.

nostalgia and design

above Nostalgic items can work well with modern furniture; here photographs of the Beatles and a willow cricket bat recall England in a Hong Kong interior.

right It is quite possible to duplicate elements in Morris Lapidus's 1950s Miami Beach apartment; for example, the curtains are bamboo blinds hung sideways.

far right Leopard-spotted velvet transforms a simple stool and its surroundings into an *Out of Africa* vignette.

There is nothing more secure than the familiar. It is true that it does sometimes breed contempt, but often this is short lived. There is a widely held view that expects every fashion to be reviled within a dozen years, open for reconsideration after another dozen or so, and apt to be a classic in twice again that timespan. Not everything makes it back at the same moment or even into widespread use, and it is nostalgia that informs our individual choices regarding what from the past will be part of our present.

Nostalgia is by definition a personal matter. It is the point of collision between the generalized past and our own, for it encompasses yearnings for something often perceived as unrecoverable, and often never originally part of our lives. Nostalgia is an emotion understood and exploited by marketing departments around the world. Suggestions that we can recreate the good life from days of yore abound in products and the promotions that surround nostalgic designs.

Although the taste for the nineteenth century is on the wane (at least those visual aspects of it that were expressions of gung-ho expansion, colonialization and industrialization) one example evoking that period illustrates the power of nostalgia. It is the world's bestselling tableware design, 'Old Country Roses'. A nineteenth-century-looking pattern actually designed at Royal Albert (a division of Royal Doulton) in 1962 and featuring the then contemporary colours of warm red, orange and pink, it has

remained unchanged to this day, and more than 100 million pieces have been sold. At the time of this pattern's release its resonance derived from a contemporary 'twist', in this case the colours. Pinpointing the exact reasons for its subsequent popularity is impossible, but 'old' and 'country' were certainly opportune choices for the design's name. The old-house look (a broad blend of colonial and later styles) has supporters in *This Old House*, continuously aired on American television since 1977 (and now shown in Britain and Korea, too), and *The Old-House Journal*, which sells house plans to its 300,000-plus readers. Country, its more 'folksy' counterpart, has appealed to a large slice of the American market with the help of Mary Emmerling,

ever since her 1980 book, *American Country*, made her name synonymous with this style. These words – 'old' and 'country' – epitomize the abstract side of nostalgia: not my past, but *the* past.

Abstract nostalgia also attaches to people, particularly those who represent a particular time or point of view. Here we enter the world of film stars and pop stars, royalty and sporting heroes, people we may have seen but, as a rule, have never met. This kind of nostalgia can catch up with living designers. Those who endure, sometimes catch on in a new way, with a new generation of consumers, or as a result of different attitudes among younger colleagues. Examples range from 'elders' Tony Duquette and Morris Lapidus to the younger but long-experienced Simon Doonan, described as the window dresser *par excellence*, whose cheeky Christmas windows at Barneys, in New York City, have created a nostalgia of their own.

Duquette was discovered by Elsie de Wolfe in the 1940s, when he was a window dresser in Los Angeles. He became known for his eclectic, sumptuous style through interiors for clients including Mary Pickford, Elizabeth Arden and J Paul Getty, and the sets for the movie *Kismet* and the original 1960 stage production of *Camelot*. Now in his eighties, Duquette is back in fashion. His LA home, Dawnridge, was the location for the spring 1999 Gucci advertising campaign. Dawnridge was anachronistic when it was decorated in the mid-1980s. Today it seems perfectly attuned to the times: Asian objects, European antiques and studio props rub shoulders on leopard-spot-covered floors, while above are chandeliers made from plumbing supplies, elk horns, pearls and a disco ball, or pink plastic cups.

The architect Lapidus, approaching 100, designed the most influential shop interiors in the interwar USA, introducing expansive plate-glass windows, theatrical interior lighting and

left In the retro home of two of the Australian design team, Dinosaur, a Bertoia chair of 1952 sets the tone; the 'woggle' sculpture is covered with 1970s wallpaper.

what Lapidus created, too. Born of Russian immigrants in a New York City ghetto, it was the whirling, colourful world of the fun fair at Coney Island that ignited his imagination and inspired the neon signage, mirrors, up-lit frosted ceilings and indirectly lit niches that Lapidus championed.

Just as some people become icons, some objects project universally understood ideas. They do so by being little able to evoke anything *but* what they stand for. Architect-designed chairs incorporating a metal structure are a prime example. Their sculptural qualities, simplicity and pedigree declare them to be evidence of modern, progressive ideas. Materials and function can be critical in other instances, too. The dark

details including curves, colour and cut-out 'woggle'-shaped recesses. Yet in 1954 his by then mainly 'less-is-more' colleagues disparaged his first large-scale building, the Miami Beach hotel, the Fontainebleau; despite its commercial success, the establishment was equally scathing about the second, the Eden Roc. He worked on against the trend, designing what may be the first pedestrian shopping mall, also in Miami, in 1960. The apartment complex he still lives in was built a year later. By then his style had been renounced as kitsch. His retort came in the form of his autobiography, entitled *Too Much is Never Enough*. Coming out of retirement in recent years, in 1999 and 2000 he was the subject of numerous magazine and newspaper features, and he was honoured by the Cooper-Hewitt National Design Museum, New York, for his lifetime's achievement. Nostalgia had played a part in his rediscovery. The stylish commercial architecture he did so much to develop was an influence on Hollywood designers at the time, and has been since. As a result the style now epitomizes the 'modern main street' that evokes wholesome but chic family-centred days and is a present-day influence in shops, restaurants and interiors. Nostalgia shaped

willow cricket bat is an unquestioned emblem of the days of the British Empire; the plump, slightly squat leather-upholstered club chair is redolent of those gentlemanly 'fat cats'. A wooden chair in eighteenth-century French style suggests elegance and hand workmanship as strongly as an original example.

Nostalgia-laden objects need to be selected with care. Too many, and too conflicting might lead your visitors' minds astray. At the very least the effect would be akin to listening to all your favourite songs at the same time.

above left and below Nostalgic chairs will often set the tone of an interior; this Mies van der Rohe version of his 1929 'Barcelona' chair (above left) would make a modern retro statement, while the elegance of the mid-century storage jars is highlighted by the setting of the nearby eighteenth-century, French-style wooden chairs (below).

retro chic

above and right In a modern retro interior (above) by architect, Ian Chee, a Warhol is partnered with a classic 1950s' sofa by the American sculptor and designer Isamu Noguchi; in contrast, a retro chic kitchen (right) employs gloss paint, fabrics, an inexpensive 'ice cream parlour' chair and a plastic-coated table to create an optimistic mid-twentieth-century mood.

In both architecture and interiors, Post-modernism took its ideas from all periods and all cultures. It also gave rise to a new kind of thinking, in which different forms of cultural understanding were accepted, producing multiple and conflicting truths. Now, in an era when interconnected and information-laden media make reality and beauty much harder to define, a distinctively 'millennium' style has arisen: retro chic. This has a range of manifestations, as we shall see, but the irony of retro chic is its determined rejection of the 'anything-means-anything' stance of Post-modernism. Instead it favours objects that display their theoretical underpinnings. Retro chic places at centre stage the modernist designs that speak optimistically of democracy, of mass-production, of new ideas and of new materials.

Retro chic is a nostalgic style that is nevertheless thoroughly of today. Even in its purest form – modern retro – it does not seek to recreate the past, but instead to reintroduce the certainties that can be found in modernist objects designed between the

mid-1920s and the early 1970s. As the Canadian-born, London-based curator and retro-modernist Neil Bingham has declared, 'The essence of modern retro is twentieth-century household items such as furniture, lighting and soft furnishings, plus those innumerable useful and decorative items that stamp the individuality of the owner on an interior.' Most of these owners are collectors, although many would deny this rather grand status, preferring to say they simply like to acquire good pieces from the modern period. They are knowledgeable about historical styles and developments within Modernism, recognize the classic pieces of each period and know how and where to acquire them. 'Individual' and 'classic' are key words in this style. Their meanings necessitate acquiring some knowledge, since the owner's recognition of the authenticity of a piece as the secret ingredient. This connects an abstract admiration of the not-so-distant past with the present-tense act of expressing personal taste.

Technology has opened up the opportunities for everyone to understand and acquire modernist furniture and objects. Internet search engines and virtual interiors, the latter presented by furniture manufacturers and auction houses alike, allow a wide range of items to be located and 'tried out' in a simulated interior prior to purchase. Book publishers, galleries and museums have also acknowledged the growing interest in mid-twentieth-century Modernism. Of late there has been a focus on well-known designers of influence – such as the husband-and-wife teams Charles and Ray Eames and Robin and Lucienne Day – as well as coverage of lesser-known but rediscovered icons, such as Maxime Old, a French designer active from the 1930s to the 1980s, and general

below The legacy of mid-twentieth-century organic forms can be seen put to creative use in Ron Arad's 'Bookworm' (1994) and Matthew Hilton's 'Balzac chair' (1991) and 'Flipper table' (1989).

studies of the period and its features. Italian and Swedish glass, ceramics of all kinds and European and American textiles play a part in this new 'take' on Modernism, but it is the chair that has taken pride of place, surviving changes and trends in fashion, continuing to look contemporary.

Some mid-twentieth-century modern furniture, such as Old's, was always intended to be custom made; perhaps the best-known luxury item is Mies van der Rohe's polished-steel-and-leather chair,

the traditional French bergère, designed by Le Corbusier, Charlotte Perriand and Pierre Jeanneret in 1928. Typically upholstered in leather (although the originals were fabric-covered), well-stuffed, square-edged cushions are contained by an exposed metal frame. Available today in both authorized and unauthorized versions, their names – 'Grand Confort Petit' and 'Grand Confort Grand' – go some way towards explaining their long-lived appeal. Le Corbusier was intent on human wellbeing and, with a handful of

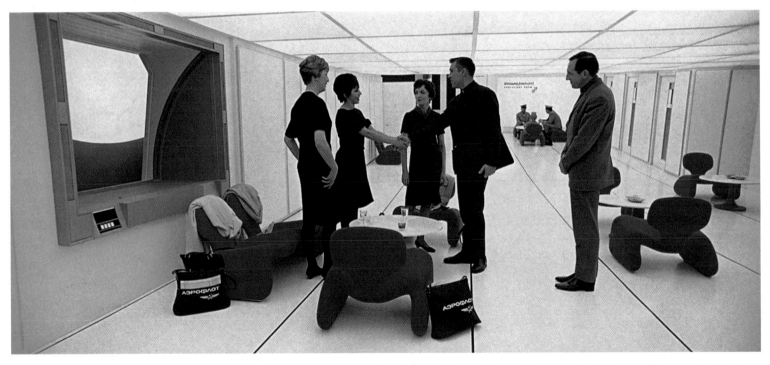

above A still from Stanley Kubrick's 1968 film, *2001: A Space Odyssey*, shows the Olivier Mourgue 'Djinn' furniture that has since become a modern retro classic.

called 'Barcelona' after the location of the German exhibition pavilion at which it

other modernist designers, he did succeed in creating furniture that combined comfort and ease with, at the same time, maintaining a sense of stylish utilitarianism.

was first seen, in 1929. The 'Barcelona' chair is still being made today, as are Marcel Breuer's 'Cesca' chairs, (see page 5) of bent metal tubing that was developed in the 1920s while he was working for Thonet, the Austrian maker of the classic bentwood chairs. Breuer cantilevered chairs made the transition from hand assembly to mass-production only in the 1960s, when they became the mainstay of many modern dining rooms. Also from the pre-war period are the well-loved large and small variants of

Since the original concept of modernists was to make well-designed things available at a reasonable price through mass-production, evidence of success lay in the continued manufacture of some postwar designs, which made full use of machine-processed plastics, fibreglass, resins, tubular steel and other new materials. Among the best known are Harry Bertoia's wiremesh 'Diamond' chairs, first made by Knoll International in the early 1950s, and Arne Jacobsen's moulded plywood 'Series 7' chairs, made since the mid-1950s by the Danish furniture manufacturer Fritz Hansen. Others are the 20 Eames pieces available through the Herman Miller Furniture Company, which from 1946, issued chairs that became synonymous with 'public' modernity: Eames's stacking, moulded-plastic 'Shell' chairs furnished entire universities or libraries and his winged plywood chairs filled countless offices. George Nelson, responsible for Miller's design policy throughout this period, was himself a prolific and influential designer, in 1948 creating what was probably the first 'stylogue' (catalogue sold as both a promotion and inspiration). His 1947 'Ball' clock – its thin, black metal-rod hands ending in a spherical knob – illustrates the range of options open to present-day seekers of the retro chic: it originally retailed for $22, goes for more than $1,000 at auction, and yet re-issues can now be purchased for $275.

To be 'in the know' is an aspect of modern retro, but not essential to retro chic. Shop fittings and media images of mid-twentieth-century modernism promote its optimism without reference to designers or the precise date of conception, as in American television shows such as *That Seventies Show*, launched in 1999 and employing props of mixed dates, or *Frasier*, with a set including an Eames ottoman and footstool of 1956 and in production ever since. Television commercials at the end of 2000 featured chairs and sofas by Bertoia, Jacobson, Nelson and others. A silhouette of Jacobsen's 1957 'Egg' chair overlaid 1970s images in a shoe-shop commercial, evoking nothing more specific than a trendy and egalitarian nostalgia. All this is far from the futuristic qualities many of the era's designs originally projected, literally with Olivier Mourgue's sculptural 'Djinn' furniture, introduced in 1968 with Stanley Kubrick's *2001: A Space Odyssey*. Nevertheless, Mourgue's chairs

above The decor for Sephora, at the Rockefeller Center, New York City, uses key elements of retro chic – notably zebra stripes, organic forms and crisp colour contrasts – to stunning effect.

also epitomized a continuity that seems increasingly sought-out today; his tactile and curvaceous forms owed a debt to the then recent past and to the organic seating created in the 1940s and 1950s by artists such as Isamu Noguchi. Furniture indebted to such organic forms appeared increasingly in the 1990s and more recently has been juxtaposed to skins of all kinds, a pairing played with in the postwar decades, too. These trends suggest a new and healthy lack of concern for what is 'in' or 'out'. The emphasis is instead on a relaxed reassessment of mid-twentieth-century designs that were themselves about stylish convenience and comfort, offering a fixed currency amid today's plethora of shifting values.

mixing and matching

above A David Gill arrangement of interwar pieces demonstrates the quirky results of juxtaposing avant garde and retrospective styles.

right Casual mixing and matching incorporates elements from many periods in a highly personal way, as here where the centrepiece is the classic 1956 bent plywood 'Lounge chair' designed by Charles Eames, which was originally designed for the film director Billy Wilder.

Every period offers evidence of mix-and-match decorating, driven by necessity, nostalgia or emulation, and rooms at the beginning of the twenty-first century are no different. However, today the underlying theme is often a deliberate emphasis on juxtapositions of objects of varied periods and cultures that seem to say that the entire world, and its history, is ours to know and enjoy.

Mixing and matching takes various forms. One is the combination of twentieth-century items, carefully considered as in modern retro. The next is similar but more casually accrued, with choices determined only by the desire to be surrounded by things that appeal to our personal taste. In the latter case earlier pieces are often included, even when the intention is to create a totally contemporary decor. An example is the home of Paris-based designer Jean-Dominique Bonhotal, which projects a twenty-first-century style through its use of furniture by such as Philippe Starck and Christian Liaigre; and an emphasis on mobility and versatility through the use of movable furniture, much of it on casters. Even the art is transitory, but among the ever-changing displays appear nineteenth-century marble statues and eighteenth-century etchings, as well as the more expected twentieth-century photographs. Bonhotal, it turns out, is also an admirer of the rustic yet sophisticated designs of American Shaker communities, hence his inclusion of floor-to-ceiling sliding panels of delicate oak slats, interwoven using the same technique used to make picnic baskets. His compatriot Patrice Gruffaz, known for his quirky designs for his own firm, Lieux – among them metal and rough-wood chairs with wings of chicken feathers, plates writhing with *trompe l'oeil* snakes and crystal goblets with bases enclosing red hearts – nevertheless combines these in his own home with eighteenth-and early-nineteenth-century furniture, gilded bronze urns and cloisonné vases.

Another current variant of mix and match is an exotic blend of Eastern and tribal arts with retro furniture and more up-to-date things. This wide-ranging slant on history is an angle that has also

permeated fashion in recent years. As an interior style it can be found in the Milan apartment of Romeo Gigli, who not long ago brought a Western rendition of the sari to the catwalk, and from thence into mainstream clothing stores. A North-South exchange has left other trends in interiors. Designers such as Luis Barragán have given Modernism a sense of place and a connection with the past, in his case bringing the vibrancy of often temporarily coloured peasant dwellings in Mexico into juxtaposition with high-style contemporary Western furniture.

Related to this type of multi-cultural blending is the increasing interest in feng shui and, more generally, in those writings that explore the contemplative 'spirit' and meaning of interiors. Compelling among the latter is Akiko Busch's account of the geography of home. Busch highlights that favourite objects – nostalgic, traditional artefacts such as a Shaker table, a wicker rocker, old tins from France, and so on – stir our affections by bringing a sense of history with them and, in our chaotic world, support the graceful coexistence of technology and nostalgia, typified by his own children watching *Terminator* films on a television set that is housed in a Shaker-style cabinet. 'There is a certain post-modern charm to that. But such confusions can also be more jarring. We tend to reject the formal ceremony of the dining room and put the computer on the dining room table, or sort the laundry there. Then, missing the sense of ritual in our lives, we turn to the ceremonies of Native Americans or Tibetan monks.'

Such incongruitites, Busch acknowledges, can confuse our lives, but they 'are also the very basis for finding comfort at home. If anything, where we live can be a place that celebrates and thrives on these incongruities that have, in one way or another, been gracefully resolved.' That resolution is found not in logic, but in the idiosyncratic and personal choices that urge us towards material expressions of both past and present as an antidote

to the intangible world of microchips, cyberspace and virtual reality. Such combinations can be found even in unlikely settings. In American baseball, for example, the new stadia in Baltimore, Cleveland, Houston and San Francisco were designed to include locality-specific quirks to make them the antithesis of the so-called 'cookie-cutter' stadia of the 1960s and 1970s. Yet my baseball-fan friends assure me that nostalgia operates only up to a point – the facilities themselves, despite the trappings, are entirely modern.

above This eclectic array has a religious theme, suggested by the 'celestial' blue plates and paint, and confirmed by the stained glass and vase.

right Simple sculptural shapes allow plastic and wood to work well together; here they also showcase a Victorian stained-glass window.

Everywhere there appears to be a consensus of opinion about how to resolve our interiors, irrespective of the taste in question. Mary Emmerling's most recent *American Country* book urges that an assortment of chairs and sofas of contrasting periods and styles is more inviting than the coordinated 'furniture-showroom look', and that unmatched furniture is not only more casual but more fun. Meanwhile Christine Kröncke, in Germany something of an interior-design institution for her pared-down but lived-in interiors, sums up her approach as a combination of 'romance and zeitgeist': 'No one thinks twice today about sitting a designer lamp on a battered hand-me-down chest of drawers, or setting a contemporary table

with their opulent family porcelain. We've come to accept that variety is amusing – and what amuses, pleases.' Taste itself is open to questioning, a fact nowhere more evident than on the September 2000 cover of *Architectural Digest*, which – unusually – illustrated four completely different rooms, from rustic to minimalist and lightheartedly retro to authentically historical. One of these, by Victoria Hagan, contains a wealth of classical references but also photographic seascapes by Hiroshi Sugimoto and furniture and objects of many different periods to 'create what she calls "a dialogue" between the pieces in a room, such as the 1940s gilt-and-metal chair and the Empire-style table in the master bedroom or elsewhere the white 1960s fibreglass chair juxtaposed with the classical fireplace.' Seeing each room as a work in progress, Hagan remarked upon the movement of objects from

one room to another: 'Everything has been everywhere. I enjoy the playful quality of looking at all the possibilities.'

Versatility, mobility and fun underpin today's blending of a mixture of periods and styles. Yet there is a serious side, for the same combination is a telling representation of the world's subtlety and complexity. At once sensuous and sophisticated, vicious and civilized, self-interested and principled, the combination of things old and new, Eastern and Western, attempts to integrate all of these worldly aspects into a coherent whole. In the most austere expressions of modernist and minimalist architecture the ideal was to free the occupants from attachments. Today mixing and matching, and making the rules up as we go along, provide the pleasing, comfortable and spontaneous interiors we seek, while at the same time answering the present-day desires for continuity, stability and a well-rounded, healthy connection to our small world. Making these links is the key to personalised decorating, which allows a handful of nostalgia-laden elements to set the tone.

left The bold geometry of its treatment allows a thoroughly modern kitchen, designed by Max Clendinning and Ralph Adron, to sit happily beneath a ceiling with Empire-period details in their Umbrian home.

finding your favourites

Adrian Mibus

Adrian Mibus is a man who is entirely immersed in twentieth-century art and furniture. His London home is constantly changing, as new items are found and others are sold to clients of Whitford Fine Arts, of which Adrian is director. Despite the fact that these interiors sometimes function as a gallery, they are also second home to an energetic young son, who has grown up romping on the boxing-ring of a Memphis' bed. The occupants everyday use of this and other limited-edition pieces is proof positive that even such rare and very valuable mid-twentieth-century and post-modernist furniture and collectibles can be at the same time comfortable and functional.

One advantage of many of the materials and design principles developed in the twentieth century is their durability. Steel, fibreglass, plastics and plywood all have excellent wearing qualities. The styles they are associated with have also stood the test of time. Another bonus is the way they readily harmonize with each other, even if made in very different decades. For example, Adrian now focuses on the 1960s to the present day, but he began his collecting with

right Plain shelves put the emphasis on the shapes and subtle colour variations of Mibus's collection of early plastics.

far right Probably the easiest retro chair to obtain is Robin Day's 'Polyprop', with more than 14 million made in several variations and colours since 1963.

late nineteenth-century Aesthetic Movement 'Gothic', moving on to Arts and Crafts and then Art Deco. His collection of Bakelite and early plastics dates from this last-named period, and yet their simplicity of form and colours make them perfect partners for his interior's later furniture. They are a reminder, too, of the wide range of collectible but practical twentieth-century objects. Small items such as these are excellent for beginning to collect. The investment is generally small and yet the benefits are still great. As you refine your tastes and increase your knowledge about a particular period in art history, a manufacturing process or even how best to find the items that you are after, then you are acquiring expertise that will be equally useful when tracking down larger items, such as chairs and sofas.

Some of the best mid-twentieth-century architect-designed chairs were stackable or for commercial use, and these are still relatively easy and inexpensive to obtain. Aside from those still being made today, such large numbers were supplied to schools, universities as well as other institutions that used examples can often be found through secondhand office furniture dealers. In this case knowing what you are looking for is essential, since these dealers are focused on the usability of their stock and, generally, not on who designed what. Check the condition carefully and buy nothing imperfect unless you are certain it can be

restored. At the same time it is worth looking for good desks, desklamps, tables and storage cabinets. On the other hand, if your heart is set on a particular item, dealers and gallery owners such as Adrian Mibus are always happy to keep an eye out on your behalf; if possible, agree in advance what the commission charge will be for this service.

If you enjoy the hunt but are pressed for time, all of the larger auction houses have specialized sales. Today most of their subscription services can be tailored to your personal interests, so you need no longer receive more catalogues than are necessary.

above and right His ever-changing living room illustrates Mibus' belief that top designer pieces are a good investment; he describes the Mourgue 'Djinn' chairs and, to their left, the 'Elephant Chair' (1966, by French artist, Bernard Rancillac) as 'funky yet functional, liveable with' and a perfect complement to the work of Pop artists such as Alan Jones (right, centre).

These catalogues can be worth obtaining even if you never intend to bid; they are packed with useful information and illustrations, and give an up-to-date indication of market prices. If knowing the current value of an item is of particular importance, make sure you obtain a list of realized prices, rather than relying on estimates alone. The internet offers connections to a range of these services. Galleries, dealers, auction houses and private auctions are all online. Among sites with well-established connections are eBay.com and artnet.com, the latter operated jointly between Frankfurt, Germany and New York City and representing galleries worldwide, including Whitford Fine Arts. One note of caution: it is wise to have some firsthand familiarity with a period before purchasing items from an image alone.

If your furniture needs to be robust, remember that excellent designers are at work today. Thinking creatively about the things that are made today means looking for the characteristics of earlier designer furnishings: being durable, comfortable and well made. Suppliers of new high-quality office equipment are a likely starting point; some deal only with architects, interior designers and others in the trade, but there are reliable firms that will sell to individuals. Patio furniture need not be ruled out, either; as long as it is sturdy it can be used to 'try out' a modern style and moved outside later. Check in the many warehouse stores; some also stock stylish and inexpensive dining chairs of bent plywood and tubular steel or moulded plastics. While there look out for the occasional collaboration with eminent designers such as Michael Graves, whose recently designed range of kitchenware for the American-based superstore, Target, well may be destined to become collectibles of the future.

Like their classic counterparts, new designer items can be sourced electronically. The internet is a valuable starting point and an effective search tool in locating furniture, designers, contact addresses and even inspirational ideas. Much of the fun, however, is in looking for yourself and meeting others with the same interests. This is another good reason why you should not hesitate to visit galleries and get to know their owners and staff; they are a goldmine of information and inevitably, like the Mibuses, enthusiasts themselves.

personal effects

As evidence of the general past, objects are the foremost source. In our own lives they are an even more powerful record of what we have done, thought, or imagined possible. Only the owner knows that a mass-produced mug, for instance, was an unexpected birthday present from a colleague, and that even after 30 years it will remain a reminder of the fact that life is full of surprises. Conversely, gazing at objects amassed by someone else leads us inevitably to wonder what the connections might be, what their owner is or was like, or why they were kept.

Most of the marks that man has left on the face of the earth during his two-million year career as a litter-bugging, meddlesome and occasionally artistic animal have one aspect in common: they are things, they are not deeds, ideas or words..

Glynn Isaac, **Whiter Archaeology?**, 1971 in Asa Briggs **Victorian Things** (London: B.T. Batsford) 1988

Private histories, like personalities, are the yardsticks of life. This has very little to do with contemporary styles and everything to do with personal taste. The fact that one object does not match anything else can make it all the more resonant.

opposite Private histories are brought to life by turning personal possessions into eye-catching and imaginative displays.

the real thing

above Historic houses offer a wealth of ideas for decorative treatments; here the Henry Francis DuPont Museum, Winterthur, is festively decked in greenery.

far right Mr Straw's modest Edwardian house in Worksop has been unaltered since the 1930s and is today popular among National Trust visitors.

The present-day obsession with possessions that connect us to each other, our environment and our personal past may stem from globalization. As James Surowiecki explains in *Slate* magazine: 'Innovation replaces tradition. The present – or perhaps the future – replaces the past. Nothing matters so much as what will come next, and what will come next can only arrive if what is here now gets overturned. While this makes the system a terrific place for innovation, it makes it a difficult place to live …' The internet has reshaped working and personal lives but also made us into potential competitors. With human nature loathe to surrender the safety of its small world, something else must provide an anchor in such shifting seas. Memories do this, and memories connected to objects are even better.

Some people *are* events. So 'sharing' in these cases can explain why, despite a slump in visitor numbers to traditional museums, there has been a growing interest in historic houses that present the story of an individual or family through the interiors and objects with which they chose to write and illustrate their story. Examples abound, but it is the USA that has the longest and strongest tradition of interpreting 'personality' houses, ranging from mansions such as Henry Francis DuPont's in Winterthur, Delaware, to entire communities, as at Colonial Williamsburg, in Virginia. The details of each room are altered according to the season. We relate to such interiors, in part, via the signs of continuity they contain. In other words, we see in other peoples' interiors evidence of similarities to ourselves. Despite the radical changes in household equipment and lifestyles, there are elements of function that have remained stable. Take the backdrops to heating, cooking and eating. Even in centrally heated homes a mantelpiece, or shelves that take its place, still provides a principal focus in living rooms. Emblematic of 'home and hearth', the mantel has always been a natural resting place for objects of special importance, warming to our hearts even if there is no real heat emerging.

Aside from the abstract kind of nostalgia that influences our choices, there is another type, not detached from a specific incident, person or place, but instead imbued with personal memories. Objects enjoyed in this sense are storytellers. Capable of reciting narratives that neither words nor conventional pictures can convey, they remind us of real events and genuine sentiments. We engage with the tales told by personal possessions in many ways: in public settings, when travelling, in private, and on the spur of the moment. We do so in increasing numbers, and not necessarily as consumers simply bent on acquiring more, or the latest thing.

Dining rooms are at one and the same time suggestive of gentrification, comfort and leisure. They embody a generosity of space (in the floor plan itself), income (to furnish it in style) and time (to enjoy eating in it). Although many meals are eaten at the kitchen counter, on the run, or in front of the television, the formal dining room, or area, continues to find a place. The presence or absence of such a space still marks distinction between classes of housing. It is particularly revealing because it often contains the least-used personal effects, such as 'good' china. It is often the setting in which inherited items are given pride of place; where memories and aspirations can override the practicalities of everyday life. We can see this even in the most luxurious of twentieth-century houses, such as Eltham Palace, near London, which was the 1930s home of Stephen and Virginia Courtauld. Built on to a medieval great hall, its well-documented rooms, now re-created, are furnished in sumptuous but

above This lacquered and gilded door and pink leather-covered chair are part of the sumptuous Art Deco decor to be seen in the formal dining room at Eltham Palace, near London.

comfortable style. Of all the rooms in the modern house, it is the dining room that dazzles as the showiest and most 'high style' in its decor.

Watching visitors in such settings, we are struck by two things over and over again. The first is that very few people are there on their own; the second is that they talk about what they are seeing. This contrasts with traditional museums, where the atmosphere tends to be hushed. In houses the objects are accepted as representing the original owner's personality – and so more naturally precipitate a conversation. The more focused the house is on a single personality, the more readily the comments seem to flow. This is true especially of interiors

associated with statesmen who have shaped concepts of nationhood, so bringing to the surface a rich combination of abstract and personal memories as well as reinforcing those associated with events.

The chatter in historic houses often centres on actually imagining living in the particular setting. It is pure curiosity, the same sort that we apply to our friends' houses. In interiors open to the public we can simply be more overt about it. In so many overhead conversations, what seems to be happening is the comparing of attitudes, taste and memories. What we take away from such visits is thus shaped as much by the people who accompany us as by the objects on display. Whatever new information we have gleaned about our companions is nevertheless a result of the environment. Objects, place and event have helped forge another link in a personal relationship.

In private spaces the sharing of responses to objects acts in the same revealing way but, in this more intimate setting, is more telling. Think of how easy it is to admit to disliking something in a museum; think then of criticizing someone's home, a favoured possession, the addition of something new or a rearrangement of objects. When personal taste and tact are at odds we reveal even more about ourselves. Our response may well become part of the story that the object in question ever-after recounts to its owner, demonstrating the ease with which complex histories – incorporating our own associations and the responses of others – can be caused in even the humblest of things. Such memories are what give objects a real past. This, in turn, makes them a vital element to include in any interior that is intended to 'speak' of a welcoming and comfortable home.

above The inclusion of personal items makes a display unique; here Winston Churchill's hats are set out poignantly amid other possessions in his much-loved home, Chartwell, Kent.

left Bullahuset, the first house in the Norwegian 'Dragon Viking' style, was built in 1860 for the violinist Old Bull; untouched since his day, it is one of many 'personality' houses that demonstrate how simple items such as photographs add character to a room.

family treasures

It has been said that few people have their homes decorated in exactly the way they would want. Although this can be for financial reasons, it can also arise – and often does – because their rooms contain things handed down from older generations. In these cases there is little use in cursing our ancestors, or wishing they had acquired magnificent furniture, paintings and property to hand on. Far better to understand the appeal of family treasures (and recognize that large and elaborately furnished houses present problems of their own) and incorporate them into a sympathetic surrounding.

The ties we have to family objects often have obvious meanings. Such things represent our roots. The most evident expression of this comes in the form of old family photographs and portrait paintings, which have long been a backdrop to living. 'Family' is, of course, as likely to embrace people who are not truly related. Images of friends, role models and benefactors were and still are often included too; the sum total is thus a daily reminder of those to whom we owe allegiances of one kind or another. More subtle meanings emerge from the way they are arranged. Formality is suggested by displaying them in orderly fashion individually framed, and hung on the wall. Their opposite alternatives – higgledy-piggledy arrangements, grouped images within one frame or displays in desktop fashion – produce a less dominating effect through informality, and this may well explain why the latter is regularly chosen for pictures of and drawings by children. The display may also itself be part of the memories evoked by such images. One of my favourite encounters in recent months was with the cousin of a friend who revealed that as a small boy he thought the floor-to-ceiling arrangement of family pictures by his grandmother was done so that the 'small people' could see their same-aged cousins and the 'big people' theirs. It turned out that the extended family was so large and his grandmother felt so committed to hanging a picture of each member, that the original decor – with the photographs only above the hallway dado rail – simply grew downwards with each successive generation. Despite this discovery, his original delight with the effect of her display was the motivation for a floor-to-ceiling arrangement years later in his own home.

After photographs, the next most common memento of generations past is china. It is good luck if an entire set has survived, but not at all unusual when it has not, which means it languishes in a cupboard or is used, mixed with other china, or displayed. The time-tested way to enhance such mixtures is to

above Objects with a common theme can be placed anywhere; here a hall chair is enlivened with a bowl of croquet balls, both in their different ways suggesting a country house past.

above The casual arrangement of simple frames suits informal portraits displayed by George Bernard Shaw in his home from 1906–50, in Ayot St Lawrence, Hertfordshire.

opposite The formality of framed oils is relieved by a more casual scattering of objects; this inviting area is in Syon House, the London home of the Duke of Northumberland.

bring them together by way of arrangement. Tightly grouping objects on a mantelpiece or shelves, or layering them in a table setting, has the effect of rendering them into a decorative whole. This treatment can be applied to other things. Similarly framing a wide range of photographs is another way to reduce disparities, although separating a photograph or painting from its original frame is not something to be decided upon in haste. Small objects, precious for their associations but not suitable – or liked – for use or mixture with other things, can also be 'framed' in wall-mounted glazed boxes, secured in glass storage jars or placed in a bowl.

influences, including books and magazines. For example, the young British illustrator Laura Stoddart brings together flea-market and junk-shop finds – from shoes to first-aid boxes – with things salvaged from her family home in a way she describes as cluttered but tidy, bunched together on white shelves or across white walls. Her impetus, she says, was that she spent her childhood reading her mother's early copies of *The World of Interiors* and old Habitat catalogues, which taught her 'how to connect things that don't necessarily relate. Those double-page spreads of teacups and tape measures and driftwood, the way things were arranged, were nectar.' Hers is not an isolated instance. Between about 1895 and 1915 the fashionable neo-Empire style bore a strong resemblance to children's books of the early 1870s, such as those illustrated by Walter Crane. This is further evidence of the way in which in our interiors we often recreate the scenes that typically captured our early imaginations.

Bedrooms and kitchens are the strongest source of childhood memories, and make them obvious locations for treasured possessions. Kitchen shelves and dressers are natural homes for inherited pottery and china, photographs and drawings, but need not be limited to these. The associations any family-linked object carries can be as sustaining as the food prepared within their sight; by providing psychological nourishment they are equally enriching of our lives. Whether kitchen counter or desk, the place where thoughts are composed, correspondence is written and telephone calls are made also invites reminders of who we are and where we came from.

above Radically different pieces work well together if they are juxtaposed with confidence; here a neo-rococo sofa gains a retro chic look with the addition of skin-like cushions.

Even items from markedly different styles and periods can be brought together in these ways, simply by juxtaposing them with confidence.

Highlighting a particular colour or material aids the blending of objects that are seemingly radically dissimilar, but if they really are at variance with each other the solution may well rest in a memory. Many of our tastes are formed in childhood, not by the style of the furnishings surrounding us, but by other visual

Bedrooms are above all sanctuaries, and so often become the resting places of things that have the greatest meaning. Here we can feel especially freed from the conventions of hospitality and function, and put anything anywhere. This is the spot to put a beloved piece of furniture that seems to fit in nowhere else. In my own case it is a tallboy that had been my father's. It came to me for temporary storage and, not liking its style, I initially looked

forward to the day when it would go. Then one day, as I was opening and closing a drawer out of curiosity, the hanging brass pull clinked loudly against its backplate. That was it. With that sound my childhood was evoked; it was the first noise I heard every morning, faintly, from the time I was born and on for another eighteen years. It is true that I built a recess for it so that it is less evident in the bedroom, but it is nevertheless there to clink for me whenever I wish to recall the simplicity and optimism of my childhood days.

Someone else may well have actually liked the look of this chest of drawers, and have enjoyed owning it for that reason, but instead it resides where it does solely because of the memories it evokes. As with all family treasures, it is the fact that we alone can hear all that the objects have to tell – visually, emotionally, or psychologically – that makes them such warming and welcoming additions to a home.

foreign treasures

above Morvi, a Gujarati palace built in 1931, shows the cosmopolitan lifestyle of its owner in its furnishings, including this Art Deco Bakelite dressing table.

opposite The Chinese Pavilion at Drottingham Palace, built for Sweden's Queen Lovisa Ulrika in 1753, shows how relatively plain materials can add exotic touches.

Since objects are a potent record of deeds, ideas and dreams, things from foreign lands encapsulate many of history's most adventurous of these, representing successive centuries of exploration, exchange and communication. Whether travelling to us or acquired when we have travelled to them, objects made in one culture and used in another reveal the shifting meanings things can convey. Deemed practical or traditional in one setting, the same item can be transformed into something decorative or novel by a change of environment. Appreciated for its visual impact, as a memento of a journey, or for the skill and knowledge it represents, a foreign treasure is thus transformed, becoming part of the entirely personal tale that our possessions tell.

There are many instances in the past when we have used foreign treasures to define who we are. Chinoiserie, a Western incorporation of Oriental objects and decorative treatments, was evidence of a privileged and sophisticated lifestyle for much of the late seventeenth, eighteenth and nineteenth centuries. So rare and costly were Chinese porcelains, lacquer boxes and screens, and handpainted silks, that the surviving examples of pre-1860s Orientalist interiors or decor are to be found exclusively in European royal and aristocratic residences. Even here, though, there were occasions when this style was more than an expression of the fashion for the exotic. In Sweden's Drottingham Palace, for example, Queen Lovisa Ulrika's Chinoiserie summer retreat, a gift to her in 1753, was a reminder of her native Prussia, where her brother, later Frederick the Great, had built a Chinese-style summerhouse at Rhensburg. In this case her taste for Chinoiserie was expressed in objects that arrived via France and so had been interpreted in the rococo spirit of the age; nevertheless, her emotional connection to them derived less from their original or transitional countries and far more from the family ties evoked both through memories and the act of receiving.

Similar scenarios can be found in interiors today. An old Caucasian camel saddlebag hangs in my Californian home, related visually to nearby objects only by its display of skilful weaving. Gazing on it, I seldom muse about its native region, which I have never seen. Instead, it conjures up Europe and similar objects in collections, both public and private, because it was given to me there by a mentor and friend, a fine weaver in her own right. Even so, I am aware of its international associations – Caucasian, Swiss, English and Californian – and like that resonance, too. Were my attitude observed by an anthropologist or sociologist, they might well conclude that for me this saddlebag is, as Daniel Miller puts it, 'the concrete means by which the contradictions held within general concepts such as the domestic or the global are in practice resolved in every-day life'. Using objects and design styles from other cultures, which are not native to us but represent something inherent in our nature – a skill, an abiding interest, or familial ties – can blend multiple meanings, 'other' and 'us', in a positive way. As Miller goes on to explain: 'one of the key struggles of modern life is to retain both a sense of authentic locality, often as narrow as the private sphere, and yet also lay claim to a cosmopolitanism that at some level may evoke rights to global status.'

than Indian. There is no reason to suppose Western attitudes dominate within these buildings, but every reason to imagine a Westerner might well feel comfortable within these interiors, recognizing familiar furnishings and arrangements of objects. The same holds true in reverse. The presence of foreign things in Western interiors – already historically indebted to distant or ancient cultures through conventions in the use and ornament of objects – speaks of an open door, telling visitors that by some route, however circuitous, we feel connected to another place and the richness of its indigenous culture.

There is little doubt, however, that direct acquaintance with another culture is the quickest route to understanding and appreciating its similarities and differences. Although importers and internet shopping make obtaining foreign items easier than ever today, a firsthand purchase has numerous benefits. Having seen where and how it was made, we have avoided the trinkets produced by sweated labourers paid unfair wages. Observation of the environment from which an object comes increases the likelihood that it will allow us to express – or discover – our own interests. This might well lay the foundation for a collection, as happened to the American sculptor Joel Shapiro, whose interest in Southeast Asian stone carvings began when, as a young man, he spent two years in south India in the Peace Corps. Travelling beyond our own territory also allows us to learn from things we never own. In recognition of this, there are a growing number of 'art' hotels around the world, containing location-specific works to be enjoyed in intimate settings.

Foreign things are not limited to the ethnic, but include art forms whose original intentions translate well across cultures. The work of many Latin American artists and artisans, for example, explores themes such as memory and the making and preserving of a collective sense of history, ideas equally meaningful and at home elsewhere. Indeed the Miami-based Cuban artist José Bedia collects African, Native American, pre-Columbian and Oceanic

above Handcrafted items – African beadwork chairs, Moroccan pierced-metal frames, an Indian carved wooden cow's head and wax-resist cloth – bond well with painted and distressed surfaces in this French interior.

Foreign treasures can bring our first insight into ways of living other than our own, and thus be gateways to becoming true citizens of the world. Objects often lose their original meaning outside their own culture, and it is this that enables us to overlay so readily meanings of our own. Yet at the same time our ownership of these items acknowledges the existence of other cultures. This current of cultural reinterpretation runs both ways. Taking India alone as an example, there one can find palaces in styles ranging from neoclassical to kitsch, villas in Italian and French tastes, manor houses inspired by British originals and chalets more Austrian

left By placing examples of folk art on a white wall, the emphasis automatically falls on the unique shape of each piece.

below This group of diverse metal objects, including an Italian bronze and an Indian silver lamp, evoke a grand tour; the patterned wallpaper – based on an early-eighteenth-century silk with a so-called 'bizarre' design – mutes the edges of each piece and becomes part of the rich ensemble.

arts to learn from them; for him they are like a library. Bedia's own work, based on Afro-Cuban rituals and legends, is informed by his firsthand study of the surviving tribes who make and use items like those he collects, as well as by his knowledge of the work of Cuban modernist painters such as Wifredo Lam, who once owned the carved Dan mask that now has pride of place in Bedia's collection. Other artists, such as the British painter Howard Hodgkin, select solely by looking, rather than knowing anything about the subject; Hodgkin's collection of Indian art from the 1560s to 1850s is, as a result, deemed to be one of the world's most visually exciting.

It matters little if the attraction is to an object's visual or contextual qualities, or both. Integrating these discovered treasures – whether rustic or elegant – in our homes is an exercise in quest of personal authenticity. At the heart of today's decoration, this quest is an interweaving of the examination of received ideas, the expression of our most expansive selves and the reinvention of fantasy-laden interiors – without forgetting that it is also the display of holiday mementoes.

favourite finds

Of all the personal effects that we gather around us, there is something special about 'found' objects, which can brighten our interior lives. These are the quirky, ephemeral, even short-lived elements in our homes, perhaps seasonal, often highly sentimental and always charged with meaning.

Nature provides us with what is often our first and most instinctive experience of discovering the beauty in something that crosses our path. Stones, shells, driftwood, reeds, feathers and leaves are just some of the things typically brought home as a

reminder of a leisurely walk, a romp on the beach or a woodland hike. Although deserts and beaches, fortunately, less frequently yield the variously coloured bottles once to be found, there is still often ample litter to be retrieved, for both the sake of the environment and the fun to be had with it. Among the interiors that have intrigued me is one with an entire wall decorated with old licence-number plates, each visually pleasing in its colour combination and typeface, and each additionally naming its origins as a reminder of where it was found. In another friend's home a motley assortment of old wrought ron brackets for hanging baskets are grouped together, their weathered and rusted forms pleasingly ornate.

above Altering the pace of your compositions – from cramped to well spaced out – will always add significance to a collection of favourite finds and poses questions about the links between them.

Recycled objects need not be limited to those that others have discarded; we are equally likely to discover an image of personal significance in the postcards, greetings cards, magazines and newspapers that circulate through our daily lives. Like photographs, these items are especially able to document a particular moment in time. Brief though this delight may be, it is all the more enjoyable when they are arranged in a stimulating way. The clichéd location for such displays, the refrigerator door,

is not the only place suitable for temporary exhibitions: bulldog clips suspended from a row of hooks or laundry pegs along a length of cord

above The fun of printed ephemera, such as postcards, in a wall collage is that their use can be short lived.

left Eclectic baskets and bowls prompt spontaneous and experimental displays that, when grouped together, create an ever-changing and visually stimulating arrangement.

offer the same opportunities for a constantly changing series of visually stimulating things. So do window ledges, bookshelves, mantelpieces, mirrors and walls. Choosing a single location for the amassing of favourite finds appears more deliberate than the surrender of every surface to the clutter of found objects. In the

indicative of our current interests and state of mind; collages of such items are scrapbooks of reinvention, reminders of future possibilities as much as of days gone by. Massed together they can summarize our ambitions, crystallize our longings, or simply focus our minds on what we have to do. Souvenirs that are bought rather than found are likely to enjoy a longer reign in our homes, if only because by the act of purchasing we have considered their inclusion more thoroughly.

All the natural finds, printed ephemera or inexpensive things that we acquire share a tendency towards short stays in our interiors. This makes them ideal for the quick changes that mark festive occasions or merely satisfy an urge to decorate in an hour or two stolen from a hectic routine. For the dedicated there is an ever-growing supply of advice books, suggesting treatments such as holed seashells looped with ribbons and hung, tied to a tension rod like long streamers. For the more spontaneous and exceedingly busy alike, shells glued to plastic or paper bags 'speared' along a rod might be quicker and more ridiculous, which may well be the right mood for that particular week or month.

The importance of favourite finds rests not so much in what we do with them, but that we *do* do something with them. They provide virtually risk-free moments of play and experimentation, returning us briefly to the joys of childhood fingerpainting, leaf kicking and collaging of hoards of simple things. Such freedom is to be relished for its own sake, but also as the precursor to more sustained exercises in decorating, be it of an entire home or just one small part of it. Our earlier years can also offer new

above Childhood treasures need not be tucked away in the attic out of sight; here they add colour and humour to a collection of mid-twentieth-century memorabilia.

far right Many objects that were made for one specific purpose can often be adapted for another, as in the case of this dressmaker's dummy, which with a new tartan cover, has been turned into a decorative stand for hats and coats.

orchestration of an interior, visual richness derives as much from a change of pace – from dense and lively to sparse and sedate – as it does from the texture and colour of the objects themselves.

Among the ephemeral items in our homes 'accidental' souvenirs such as tickets, leaflets and travel passes have a special role to play. The decision to display that ticket to, say, Ralph Fiennes' performance in *Richard II*, is a present-tense impulse, ideas; we may well find that possessions we once put away as outgrown can once again delight us. The reasons can be many:the sense of irony or humour they convey, the value we now recognize in them, or the sentiments they embody.

Attics, cupboards, garages – or junk shops and yard and carboot sales – can yield up a wealth of objects worthy of becoming newfound favourites. My mother's garage was not long ago the site of my own most recent rediscovery: a pair of glazed earthenware candlesticks I bought cheaply for practical purposes while a student in power-rationed Edinburgh in 1971. They sit on my mantelpiece now not so much as a reminder of those days but because one is inscribed 'Dinna licht yer candle at baith ends'. Looking at them now makes me chuckle, for I see clearly how wise is the advice and how futile the hope of trying to follow it. Clearly, things that we have ourselves purchased previously, but put away, are the richest source of delight. In such objects we not only have the fun of a favourite find. Retrieved items also bring with them a sense of being reunited with an old friend, as well as a reminder of how we continue to accrue greater self-awareness with the passage of time.

Rethinking the role of objects is fundamental to being an active participant in the shaping of our destinies. On the journey through life, changes are often subtle and occur over time. Objects that have a long personal connection with us are natural choices to represent this continuity, but ephemeral items are equally important, being symbols of spontaneity, surprise, flexibility and reassessment. These are constant aspects of our existence that allow enjoyment of the small things in life, hone our creative skills, reflect upon our actions and judgements. Just as a good journal records the daily discoveries and observations that make us who we are today and tomorrow, the rearrangement and reassessment of things important to us reflect our growth and changes in beliefs, emotions and hopes. It is an exercise well worth undertaking often, for it is bound to be revealing.

finding the right image

Sue Timney and Grahame Fowler

Sue Timney and Grahame Fowler are internationally known design consultants who supply their expertise to leading fashion and household-product manufacturers such as Ann Klein, Martex, Dunhill, Wedgwood, Cerutti and Etro. They also produce and distribute high-quality wallpapers and furnishing textiles under their own names, and have most recently expanded into the American market. The wit and style they bring to their work is reflected in their private collections, which in turn have provided the inspiration for the colour schemes and decorative details that can be found in their home.

Sue Timney started collecting ceramics about 20 years ago, when she was at college. Both are graduates of the Royal College of Art, where Sue studied fine art and Grahame textiles and graphics, and since then they have worked together as Timney-Fowler, founded in 1979. At first Sue collected only black-and-white pieces; it was their range of boldly scaled black-and-white printed furnishing fabrics, launched directly to the public through their first shop, which opened in London in 1983, that took the partnership into

right The wall behind the bed has a varied montage of family photographs, with a larger frame for the central portrait acting as a focal point for the arrangement.

above far right These cushions, covered with fabrics from Timney-Fowler's Cinquecento range, shows how an unusual fabric can inspire a decorative scheme.

the limelight and their designs into museums. The style that made them famous was based on witty revamps of engravings from neoclassical design and architectural source books: giant Roman emperor's heads, not-to-scale combinations of late seventeenth-century urns and drapes, or details from a patternbook for stonemasons and woodcarvers. Until the mid-1980s their collections retained that startling purity of a black-on-white, copperplate style, but within a few years they had moved on to explore the warm, multi-coloured palette – and imagery – of Italian cinquecento paintings.

Long-time residents of west London, they recently decided to move next door to have the challenge of refurbishing a house from scratch. In the final version their well-honed eye for old prints, photographs, ceramics and furniture has been put to use with their own fabrics and wallpapers to create a haven of inspiration. Every room has a collection of objects that suggested a starting point for the decoration. The focus in the strongly coloured living room is provided by the bright 1950s and 1960s ceramics, selected solely for their striking shapes and patterns. Some of Sue's favourite pieces were found in junk shops or at jumble sales; others came from antique shops. The inspiration for

above Sue Timney's collection of mid-twentieth-century ceramics was the inspiration for the dramatic colour scheme in the living room, where black paint emphasizes the architectural features.

right The broad, horizontal, patterned hinges on an oak cabinet provided the idea for the display of ceramics on a single high shelf in the dining area; in the hallway beyond, a Henry Moore scarf framed and hung on a horizontally striped wallpaper continues the theme.

the four colours that divide the living-room walls came from this collection. Starting from floor level, the dado is a dark red. Above that, and filling most of the wall space, is a soft chrome yellow, a colour often used in mid-twentieth-century ceramics. The frieze at the top is dove grey, another favourite of the period. The dado and picture rails are black, acting as dividing lines between the other colours and tying the room together – black being the colour for a variety of lamps and furniture.

One addition to the 1880s house was built at Timney's instigation: 'What I really craved in London was a rural feeling of living out in the country and being surrounded by trees. So I decided to build a conservatory-style kitchen-dining room, with the walls clad with reclaimed Victorian floorboards.' The framework was painted forest green to complete the effect. A collection of art plates work well in this rustic setting because their scratchlike and fine-line details are in harmony with the pronounced grain of the old wood and the texture of the African slate tiles on the floor.

A display of family photographs was the basis for a monochromatic scheme in the master bedroom, highlighted with colour accents and various shades of grey. The black frames are a perfect counterbalance to the strong geometrics of the bed and cupboard doors. Placing emphasis on the frames by the choice of black also lends a sense of rhythm to this dense grouping, making it informal and inviting. A single large frame with a wide mitred profile has been placed in the centre to act as a focal point. To enliven the colour scheme a limited range of terracotta, clay and grey tones were introduced, picking up the hues dotted throughout the photographs. These additional colours were provided by cushions covered in a mixture of ethnic and Timney-Fowler textiles and antique English blankets on the bed. The dramatic but welcoming results demonstrate how effectively a limited colour scheme and basic pattern – in this case rectangles and squares – can pull together items from very different sources.

collecting

Collections constitute an important part of our public expression of culture, forming the backbone of museum, archive and gallery displays and often providing the inspiration for new products as well as revivals of old ones. Just as they have developed and are used in a variety of ways in institutions – for example for publicity, education, or entertainment – they have parallel roles in domestic settings.

It ought to be obvious that the objects that occupy our daily lives are in fact the objects of a passion, that of personal possession, whose quotient of invested affect is in no way inferior to that of any other variety of human passion.

Jean Baudrillard, 'The System of Collecting', **The Cultures of Collecting** (London: Reaktion Books) 1994

Given the chance, every child displays the collecting instinct, in fact a hangover from hunter-gatherer traits that express themselves in curiosity and acquisitiveness. Few adults can resist continuing these habits throughout life, and if they have also developed a knack for hoarding with style, their interiors reveal their hobbies, knowledge, obsessions... and often much more.

opposite Miniatures of objects are highly collectible, and their small stature is emphasized by placing them within sight of something of normal scale.

the passion for possessions

The collecting urge captures all of us at one time or another. Whether we succumb to gathering matchboxes, jewellery, teapots or toys, the act of assembling them together is a projection of our sense of reality. Collections can paint a whole picture, represent diversity and exude a strong sense of personal identity, all at the same time. Their complexity is part of their appeal. The process is open-ended, the possibilities encompass both precious and mundane things, and the result is always unique. The intellectual or visual thread that binds a collection together is yours and yours alone.

It has been said that collecting is today a more powerful expression of our culture than either politics or religion. It is also clear that the extent to which we engage with collecting ranges from a casual interest to obsession; degrees of self-interest are the yardstick for measuring our involvement with objects. Self-interest, of course, can be both negative and positive, as we know from holistic medicine and exercise, or psychoanalysis. The latter is a particularly apt reminder of the connection between objects and character, collecting and analysis, for Sigmund Freud did both. Just prior to the beginning of the twentieth century Freud began to collect records of dreams, jokes, early memories and slips of the tongue. He collected objects from the ancient world as well, using his

above In the Freud Museum, London, we can visit Sigmund Freud's consulting room and see his collection of antiquities.

right Collecting cooking and eating implements offers endless opportunities; Natalie Hambro's open-shelf displays are connected by a focus on metals.

collecting

tangible collection as a symbol of the unconscious mind: what had been buried was what had survived. Freud believed that collecting was a substitute for an emotional or libidinal tie, likening each acquisition to a conquest. Yet, having started amassing antiquities as a result of the death of his father, he declared it to be also a source of renewal and comfort. Where our own activities sit along this spectrum depends on the emphasis: a focus on acquisition is at one end, understanding – of both the objects and, through them, oneself – at the other. Collecting is a shared and universal interest, so it offers insights into the very nature of humanity.

Collecting can begin innocently enough. Some people discover a common theme among a few objects they possess and pursue it, a tack particularly appropriate for large topics, which present a wealth of opportunities for additions. Among these the most all-embracing are linked to broad categories of human pleasures: living with animals, playing games, and cooking and eating. Narrowing down the focus may only marginally limit the

below Small similar items need to be displayed close together to emphasise their individuality, shown by these Georgian silver fish at Ickworth House, Bury St Edmonds.

collection; for example, jugs for oil were probably the most widely produced kitchen article over the past 2,000 years, while in the past 200 alone the production of an enormous assortment of things such as salt and pepper shakers, baking moulds, enamelware and painted biscuit tins and trays has provided endless opportunities for their collectors. Since it is impossible to define the limits of such categories, these appeal to hobbyists – which most of us are – who welcome the individuality of each piece, its character, its quirks and even its cracks. The decision to include or exclude a particular piece is primarily dependent on our personal response to the look of the thing. After all, if there are many to choose from, why not

choose the·ones you like? The end result is an essay on individual taste and character. Observing our own and other people"s collections can therefore reveal a great deal about the likes and dislikes that shaped their formation.

Freud's collection, on the other hand, is an example of the impulse to gather together objects that share a certain history, rather than attracting attention – initially at least – for their visual qualities. Such groupings can explain a subject, support a theory or demonstrate a particular stylistic or technical development. Many museums began as repositories for these sorts of 'explanatory' collections, which were displayed in crowded case after crowded case and, to the visual delight of dedicated hoarders, occasionally still are. The narrative retold by such objects is one, often, of progress; in this respect they are somewhat like impersonal souvenirs, in that they carry evidence of the past – how things were made, used and developed. Gathering things together to tell a history is not restricted to museums, as collectors who seek complete runs of things such as stamps, coins, dolls, train sets, cameras or baseball cards can attest. The greater the ambition to impose order, to define the first and last in the series and fill all the gaps in between, the greater the obsession. It is then that the tempering factor of self-knowledge can be a saving grace; learning from the objects can turn a one-sided acquisitiveness into a more constructive relationship.

When the focus narrows even more tightly we enter the realm of obsession, fetishism

opposite Display ideas may come from shop fittings; The Lulu Guiness shop, London, is a prime example of creativity in display.

below An obsession with Farrah Fawcett defines this New Jersey attic room, but the arrangement of magazine covers as wallpaper is relevant for any favourite images.

and intense preoccupations with the issues of life and death. Fetishism in this context is the act of seeking one's identity in objects removed from any reference to their context and history; it is a refusal to appreciate the reflection of reality they bring into our homes. Enlightened ownership, however bizarre it may appear, is far healthier than blind possessiveness. In the continuum between the spiritual and the material it is, again, enlightenment or knowledge that makes objects meaningful to us; this is the foundation of the importance

above and right A more formal variant of collage-making in interiors can be created with collections of similar things that are contained within geometric lines. This could be a parade of glassware marching in a grid-covered kitchen or alternatively a breathtaking expanse of books used as a focal point in a large room.

assigned to shrines, memorials – even snaps of our friends.

Death, or our fear of it, is acknowledged by Freudian psychologists as a prime motive for the gathering together of objects. A collection can symbolize a wish for immortality, when it is conceived as something to be handed on intact, or a desire to make someone else immortal, as often happens when rooms remain unchanged after the loss of a loved one. In these ways objects grapple with death on our behalf, acting out the roles of both allies and referees in the game that is our life. Similarly, collections remain alive only as long as they continue to grow and evolve with us; as a result, selling them is, for some people, preferable to retaining them once the group appears to be complete.

The desire to 'have it all' runs deep in our psyche. It is an emotional state that is well understood and pandered to (even

exploited) in today's shopping environment. Thanks to stores and online services, catalogues and magazines, we can see all the possibilities, all the colours available, all the time. Most people manage to contain the impulse to buy everything they see, although there are a few like Thomas Cary, whose small Manhattan apartment houses more than 50 categories of objects, from important sporting art to every James Bond-related item he can find. Far better, perhaps on the other hand, to content oneself with borrowing the tricks of shopfitters and designers, whose forte is the display and arrangement of a multitude of similar things. Observe the way scale and form is emphasized, or contrasts highlighted. Note the prominence, or lack of it, of the supporting display devices. Are the shelves eye-catching or near invisible? Is the arrangement derived from some aspect of the objects themselves, or totally discrete? Do the objects melt into the background, or appear quite separate from it through the use of lighting or reflection?

The arranging of a collection is intimately entwined with the gathering of it, through the collage-like nature of decorating itself. As explained by another contributor to *The Cultures of Collecting*, (drawn upon for the start of this chapter): 'There are certain perhaps surprising – yet quite definite – analogies between collecting in the broad sense and the modern artistic practice of collage-making.' Pointing to their shared method – creating a single statement out of a group of things – and the fact that amateurs can do both, Roger Cardinal nevertheless adds: 'dedicated collage-making, like dedicated collecting, is of rather deeper resonance… both aspire to be noticed, inspected, admired, even envied.' He might well have added that both strive to communicate. We all have stories we need to tell, stories we want to remember, and stories that, like a child with a favourite fairytale, we wish to hear over and over again. With a collection we can achieve all of these things, learning more about the past, our world and ourselves in the process of bringing it into being.

a life's work made visible

above A quirky shrine to Hoover, his late poodle, includes this wall relief of 'plastic plaster', old clothes and records, made by the London artist, David Harrison.

opposite An eye-catching focal point is made by framing an eclectic selection of fashion accessories and a jacket in Paul Smith's new London showroom.

The most individual of collections are often those that stem from a personal interest. The objects thus gathered together then become more than mere possessions. Instead they engage in a dialogue with us; they offer up information and visual stimulation while we increase their value to us through our personal use and understanding of them.

The spark that sets off a collection might be a hobby, such as gardening, music or cooking. These can lead to an interest in all manner of related things, from outdoor statuary to windchimes, tribal drums to old sheet music, or antique tureens to wire whisks. The fun of following our personal passions is that interesting mixes can emerge. Allowing objects of differing character – inexpensive and expensive, crudely made and finely executed, useful and ornamental – creates a lively, even humorous, display, as the contradictions between them generate a visual excitement. The internationally honoured French interior designer Andrée Putman recently declared: 'Your junk objects can look so good next to your official treasures.' Why? 'They educate each other. They chat. Life begins when they meet. The freedom of jumping from one period to another, creating a historical mess, appears to me as the ultimate pleasure.' But she warns that it only works aesthetically if your selection is sincere.

The link between gardens, music and food is in their making and so, by extension, collecting anything related to what we ourselves do regularly provides the same possibilities for dialogue. The embroiderer who decorates with quilts and samplers, or the enthusiastic cook who hunts down dinner menus or old recipe cards and books, are both in different ways gathering together ideas as well as objects, and inevitably can grow to appreciate otherwise overlooked, inexpensive finds. The added advantage of collecting as accessory to a passion is that it takes the focus away from buying as investment alone. This is never wise, because things are so subject to changing fashions that their monetary values can fall as well as rise. Developing collections around a personal interest can also transform the passive activities we already enjoy. Many of us take particular pleasure in watching films or sporting events, listening to music or attending performances of dance or drama. Learning more about these through the memorabilia they generate can add to our appreciation. Of course, the most ardent fans will need no prompting, but it is equally possible that a dormant passion can be kindled by the acquisition of a single film poster, an old golf club or even a stage prop.

We may well already own the beginnings of an activity-based collection. Consider the range of old rakes, trugs, trowels and the like that often remain stashed away in garages and garden sheds. Think of those LP sleeves containing loved but scratched records; emptied, they can become decorative instead of protective, and might even lead to an interest in the cover artists who created them. Whether keen sailors, sporting fishermen, enthusiastic travellers, snap-happy photographers or ardent letter writers, the informed eye we bring to our cabin bells, fishing flies and floats, postcards, cameras, photographs or pens can be the basis for a lifelong quest for other similar objects. Mundane activities can be transformed by bringing to bear the collector's eye. Seeking out old housekeeping manuals, butler's trays, brooms, or crumb plates

can transform an individual's attitude to housekeeping. Even laundering has its own devoted worldwide following, led by Jacques Lebrun, president of Eurofer, a club for those who collect things to do with washing and ironing. If the weekly shopping is a chore, keeping a lookout for limited-edition packaging can change that for ever, as happened to the Englishman who, with children in tow, discovered the ever-changing Spaghetti-O labels and has collected them ever since. These latter sort, the most ephemeral of collections, can prove the most fun of all, and yet we can discard them – or recycle them – when our lives move in another direction.

above Pinned-up visualizations of ideas, whether notes, sketches, recipes or – as at this illustrator's desk – watercolours, make a desk a more inspiring place.

right In Jacques Lebrun's Musée du Lavage et du Repassage, Verneuil-en-Bourbonnais, France, simple shelves show off his private collection of irons.

Many of the most intriguing collections are those with a strong connection to their owner's work, manifestations of a professional and private enthusiasm that enriches both spheres of a life. The most obvious links occur when an occupation is in some way related to the decorative arts, although even then the results can be remarkably diverse. For some the objects are both decoration and reference, as in the case of Peter Hone, a British authority on carved and cast architectural ornaments, which fill his London residence from top to bottom. For others the relationship is less direct. For example, the Postmodernist architect and furniture designer Michael Graves lives in a New Jersey home built by Italian stonemasons in 1926 and, in keeping both with its Tuscan villa appearance and his influential rethink of classical styles, displays within it his collection of Etruscan, Greek and Roman pottery and glass. Connected through their neoclassical lines are his examples of Biedermeier furniture, made at least sixteen centuries later, while the classicism of a *c.*1900 Viennese pot, by Josef Hoffmann, prompted Graves to display it beside an antique Tunisian vessel. The quest for these connections was personal, and is defining of Graves. 'It is the idea of something telling stories, of pieces standing in lieu of something else,' he has said. 'That's where the architecture and collection meet.' Photographer Mary Ellen Mark, on the other hand, collects black-and-white images by masters in her own field, but also anonymous souvenirs from her travels, among them Mexican

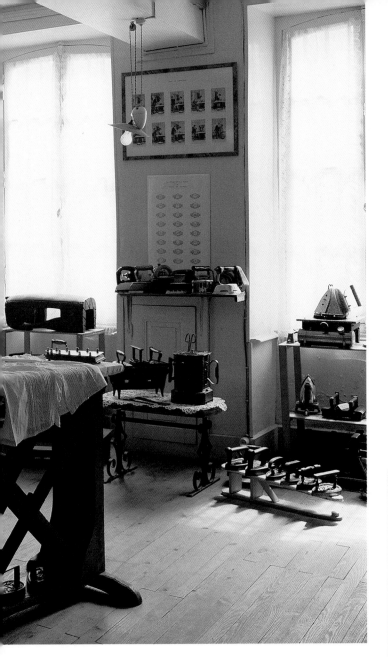

are, like Elton John and Charles Saatchi, involved in high-profile industries, and their collections are vivid examples of how objects can project a persona or lifestyle. At the opposite end of the spectrum is a collection kept in a desk drawer in a friend's home: beautifully designed 1950s boxes for paperclips, pencils and other office ephemera, gathered by his mother before she gave up her office life for home. Eloquent in its message, it poignantly projects a fascination with the trappings of a career destined to be cut short. Like many other modest collections, it works because it grew out of a personal discovery of the delight to be found in everyday things and survived intact as it clearly encapsulates its original owner's character.

below Even mundane things can form an attractive display, as proved by the well-known florist Barry Ferguson, whose collection of watering cans adds interest to a corner grouping.

animal masks, American duck decoys, Moroccan textiles, Icelandic folk art and old circus posters. What connects these two collections is that the work she is best known for is her social-documentary photography of prostitutes, addicts, famine victims and street kids – all also anonymous.

Connections between public and private selves are revealed through collecting practices and methods of display. Some can be highly visible. There are hoteliers who collect art by turning their rooms over to individual artists to decorate, as at L'Atelier sul Mare, in Sicily; there are collectors who display their treasures in exclusive hotels, such as Twin Farms in Barnard, Vermont, owned by the Twigg-Smith family, who are among the world's top private-art collectors. Many of those ranked in the top 200

collectors and their homes

It goes without saying that collections come in all shapes and sizes, and inhabit spaces both large and small. Setting those distinctions aside, though, it is possible to separate collections into three broad types, linked to the way they are displayed. There are conscious collections, massed together; there are informal collections, interspersed with other things; and there are lifestyle collections, which dominate entire homes.

Asking a range of people what the term 'collector' meant to them, I was reminded that we all have different perceptions of other people's pastimes. The answers, of course, in part reflected each individual's collecting habits, and ranged from 'granny, with all those knick-knacks in a what-not', through 'art collectors with super-stylish penthouses' to 'antique collectors and their overly decadent homes'. Categorizing these, granny is the conscious collector, the penthouse owner takes the informal approach, while the decadent has a lifestyle collection. To discover which one we may be, it is worth considering for a moment the way we choose to stash recyclables like cans, bottles and plastic or paper bags, and how we fill our kitchen shelves, store books or arrange our closets. These are clues to both our character and what type of displays will please us most. If there is a self-contained place for everything, we are probably

above 'Conscious' collections are most often multiples of similar things; together their unique features are highlighted, yet they 'read' as a unit because no other similar item could be placed among them.

right An informal arrangement of madonnas demonstrates the universal system of proportions, where their visual balance is derived from a grouping that places the focus on two small and five mid-sized examples, placed around three large figures.

grannies, in the sense that our desire for order leads us to create conscious collections, both thought of and presented as a group. If things are stored solely with convenience in mind, close at hand for the moment they are needed, we are the arty type, likely to disperse related objects around a room. Finally, if there are no closets but armoires and chests instead, or if our books are all of a period and housed in compatible fashion – be it neoclassical or modern retro – we are likely to be decadents, wishing to create a unified, all-things-considered environment.

When we know ourselves well, the objects we decide to collect will suit the method of arrangement we like best. Conscious collections are most often multiples of similar things. They might be defined by material, perhaps china, glass, silver or Bakelite, although it is equally possible that the parameters are set by function, as in the case of collections of buttons, books, boxes, keys, masks, tools, and so on. Displaying these together is logical, especially if they are small and/or very like each other, since if dispersed their minute differences will go unappreciated. Indeed if the objects in question are so small that they can each fit comfortably in the palm of your hand, they will offer no

above A spontaneous-looking focal point for an austere interior can be made from a collection of sturdy things stashed in an unused alcove or, as here in designer Dinny Hall's London home, a fireplace.

suggestion of a collection at all if they are scattered around a room. Like pot-pourri, which can only function when its various ingredients come together in a single bowl or bag, tiny things need to be tightly grouped – even contained – to be brought to life. The same is true of larger items that are identical in material and finish: handthrown, plain-glazed jugs and crocks will show off their makers' skill, spatterware and old glass will reveal their individual streaks and bubbles, and wooden boxes and slatted baskets will draw attention to their subtle differences in grain. With conscious collections such as these we have the opportunity to transform mere orderliness into patternmaking, by treating the objects like ingredients in a surface-designer's arsenal. We can experiment with positive and negative space by placing dark things on light grounds or vice versa; we can try introducing pattern behind the objects, to integrate them more completely with their setting; or we can arrange them to emphasize their textures and designs rather than their silhouettes. Best of all, we can try out many different groupings, bearing in mind only that items in a narrowly-

defined collection should be placed just close enough to each other to prevent another similarly-sized object from fitting in between them and ruining the display.

Informal collections, on the other hand, tend to be based on broad themes and do not mind sharing their space with other things. In fact, it is often part of their raison d'être to create a general ambience, rather than a focused point of interest. They might centre on modern or folk arts, take a region as their basis (and 'country' is included here), or be related through other similarly loose associations, such as texture, pattern, technique or colour. Fossils and shells, ethnic textiles and handpainted earthenware, and black-and-white engravings and photographs all function happily as informal backdrops or decorative additions. Because such collections are less narrowly defined, they also tend to be less conservative, not in terms of style but in the attitude taken towards deciding what fits and what does not. In some respects decadent collections are the most open-ended of all, in that the definition of what fits tends to be tied to a particular historical period and can therefore encompass anything at all, as long as it meets that single criteria. Here the emphasis is on creating a harmonious sense of authenticity; as a result, there may well be a complete lack of focus, since these collections take entire rooms, or homes, as their 'display cases'.

Both decadent and informal collections exhibit a great tendency to combine objects of quite different sizes. In these cases it can be helpful to consider the 1-2-3-5-8 principle that underpins a seemingly universal system of preferred proportions, found in use by Ancient Greek and Roman builders, Native American image-makers and our present-day five-by-eight glossies, to name but a few (mathematicians know this chain of numbers as part of the Fibonnaci series, which grows by adding the last two numbers to find the next). As a rough guide, it provides a starting point for harmonious groupings according to scale. The largest pieces number one, two or three, and the next two largest take the

below Articulated forms, strong colours and the gleam of wood, glass and copper items are the broad themes that pull together Jacque Grange's own dining room in Paris.

remaining of these three numbers. Smaller items then number five, or smallish items are ranged together, five being of different scale from another three or eight. As with all systems, it is only a place to begin. Objects are like puppets, brought to life by human hands but only magical if those hands are out of sight. So it is with arranging collections: the result, at best, should look natural.

In the end, whether we are aware of it or not, we are all collectors of one type or another, or even all three. The very act of participating in life requires us to remember, reflect, organize,

arrange things, plan ahead and strive for comfort and security. These are the very same skills we bring into play – and can sharpen considerably – by being attuned to our environments, starting with the ones that we create for ourselves. In this sense every home is in itself a collection, as individual as its occupants, and, like them, easy to live with if they remain open to reinvention, rediscovery and reassessment.

above Engulfing an entire wall with variously framed portraits and paintings creates a comfortably decadent setting for a multitude of other objects, here in the London home of photographer Nigel Spalding.

display and storage

Bernhard Paul

Displaying collections effectively is a challenge. Finding the right solution draws upon techniques long practised by decorators and interior designers, such as highlighting a few carefully selected items through dramatic lighting or placement. When the collection is extensive or fragile, however, the answer may well be found by looking to other related fields, such as shop and museum displays. All of these options have been brought into play in the interiors created by Bernhard Paul, the artistic director of Circus Roncalli whose collection of circus memorabilia provides decorative accents in his private apartments, as well as forming the basis of his private museum in Cologne, Germany.

When deciding where to display objects, the first consideration should be the amount of natural light falling into the room. Inert materials, such as stone, glass, metal and ceramics, tolerate light well, as evidenced by the longevity of stained-glass and exterior-tile work. Among colouring substances, glazes, lacquer and oil-based pigments fade far more slowly than water-based ones. Thus oils on canvas, lithographs on paper or tin, and lacquered or

right Old commercial cabinets form the background for Paul's main display of circus memorabilia, reinforcing the 'curio-shop' nature of his extensive collection.

far right Paul stands beside his open-shelf-and-box storage system, used for fragile and light-sensitive items; a handful of clown masks on top hint at the contents.

varnished objects (whether wood or papier mâché) all withstand light far better than watercolours, pen-and-ink drawings, and things that are stained or dyed. Aside from fading colours, light can also degrade certain materials. Those most endangered by strong light – whether natural or artificial – are textiles and paper. Silks are especially vulnerable, as are cardboard and similarly 'soft' papers used for many souvenirs, boxes and cards of all kinds. To protect such light-sensitive items, glass for windows, frames or cabinets can now be purchased with an ultraviolet barrier, or this can be applied in film form to windows. If none of these is a viable option, the lifespan of delicate objects can be extended by using diffused rather than spot lighting and positioning them in the darkest area of the room.

Particularly light-sensitive or fragile items are best stored in cabinets with shallow drawers. If wooden, these can easily have a glass 'lid' added across the top, so that each one acts as a small display case. Paul has used

above Many freestanding kitchen units, such as this Ikea example from their Varde range, are equally suited to storing collections conveniently and safely; the glass-fronted drawers mean they can still be seen.

early twentieth-century cabinets, in keeping with his collection, much of which dates from the decades either side of 1900. For objects of any other period there are equally appropriate cabinets, bookcases, dressers, plan chests or tray-on-shelf fittings to be found. One important point is often overlooked: ensure that drawers, shelves or trays will hold objects without crushing, bending or folding them. If they are shaped – perhaps fans, hats, shells, tools or toys – a yielding support, such as fabric-covered foam, provides greater protection and holds items securely in place. Individual stands are another option. As illustrated by Paul's masks, these not only create effective displays, but also allow for the rotation of stored items, thereby reducing exposure to light.

Aside from the size and shape of storage drawers, shelves, supports and frames, another critical factor is avoiding mixing certain materials together. Untreated wood and many papers and paper-based items contain harmful acids that gradually degrade textiles and paper itself. Precious metals present challenges, too, becoming tarnished by even a minute amount of fumes, such as those emitted by some old paints, varnishes, dyes and early plastics. Gilded objects can even be discoloured by the close proximity of perfumes. The solution is to frame or store things in acid-free or inert materials, to create a neutral barrier. Acid-free tissue paper and framing mounts are widely available, as are plain, soft, unbleached, undyed and washed fabrics – for lining drawers, making storage bags and covering shaped supports or shelves. If all this seems a minefield, good dealers, auctioneers and most museums will provide basic guidelines for particular materials. At the very least, by grouping similar objects together there is less likelihood of mixing incompatible materials. An additional bonus can be the visual cohesion created by amassing things that share their method of construction.

When your acquisitions are numerous and are to be tightly grouped, as is Paul's collection of decorative tins, shelving can be nondescript, to place emphasis on the highly contrasting

surfaces. There are endless choices among the many shelving and display systems available today in inert materials such as metal, glass and sealed wood. However, when modern ready-made modular systems are not in keeping with the objects – or your interiors – there are two other options. Cabinet makers and suppliers of museum-standard display cases can provide tailor-made units compatible with decorative schemes. The marginally higher cost is well worth it for the quality and individuality of the result. It is also still possible to find suitable secondhand or antique display cases, retrieved from pharmacies, haberdasheries and hardware suppliers and even galleries and museums. They can vary from clean-lined to eccentric mid-twentieth-century, or, as with Paul's old shop fittings, give a 'curio-shop' impression.

above Although varied in size, shape and details, these tins are alike in their method of construction; visual cohesion comes from not mixing incompatible materials.

opposite From his stored collection of masks Paul rotates those in his 1920s- and 1930s-style dining room, limiting deterioration through light exposure.

collecting the look

Terry Burgess and Andrew Newman

Terry Burgess and Andrew Newman seem to be a perfect pair. They both work in media, Terry as a recent presenter of Britain's television fashion programme *Slave*, and Andrew once in charge of light entertainment at Channel 4, but now at the helm of a new entertainment channel, E4. As avid aficionados of design, they have chosen to decorate their kitchen in a manner befitting the happiest of couples: mid-twentieth-century *moderne*. It is an upbeat style bound to make you feel good.

As categories of collectors go, Terry and Andrew are decadents, intent on collecting things for their kitchen that epitomize the late 1940s and 1950s. Arranged along shelves above the American diner-style table, around the period refrigerator and along the countertops, they impart the strong impression of menus, labels and other graphics that project the postwar illusion of domestic bliss. It is an interesting choice, given that, aside from her television work, Terry is also associate editor of the French fashion magazine *Self Service*, and inhouse stylist for the risqué underwear company, Agent Provocateur. Clearly not intent on emulating the

right Terry and Andrew reveal their retro-chic kitchen, created with a few key items, simple shelving and a 1950s colour for the walls and cabinets.

far right Terry's favourite item is a 1950s egg poacher, set on the stove for display rather than for actual use.

happy housewife whose image is dotted around her kitchen walls, Terry has, on the other hand, been known to hang an oven glove from her neck as a purse. It all suggests a suitably 1950s martini mixed from one measure of fetishism and an equal measure of self-mocking artfulness.

Except for the fact that these kitcheny things are placed in a kitchen, in all other respects they are divorced from their context – or at least, they appear to be displayed, like that oven glove, for their effect rather than their history. As Terry tellingly said of her 1950s egg poacher, which is the thing she loves most, 'I've never used it, but just owning it makes me feel like Doris Day.' Her obvious delight proves that old utilitarian things can be a joy to own and display when they conjure up a similarly satisfying image. The same holds true for decorative objects of any period. For example, the German-born, Paris-based couturier Karl Lagerfeld surrounds himself entirely with eighteenth-century French things because he believes that they epitomize an appropriately elegant and refined lifestyle. If a particular culture or period appeals as strongly to you, let yourself be a decadent in the Burgess-Newman mould, gathering images and objects from a single decade or two.

above Mid-twentieth-century ephemera such as menus and containers can be safely displayed in kitchens to good effect, as long as the atmosphere is not too steamy.

right Many foodstuffs available today carry images barely changed over the past 50 or so years; as with these Sun-Maid raisins, the clue to an 'authentic' label is a registration mark next to a distinctive image.

The Burgess-Newman kitchen has the hallmarks of a professionally styled interior, to be expected from a couple whose working lives are so closely bound up with visual presentation. Theirs is an undoubtedly nostalgic vision, but nevertheless the equivalent of today's high-tech kitchens with a wealth of costly gadgets, many of which remain unused (creating these types of kitchens is a recognition of that 'something soothing' in the rituals of domestic labour, even if it is only in imagining them). If gadgets are your weakness there are many available, newly made but in mid-twentieth-century style, including a selection of mixers, milkshake blenders and espresso makers. Dishcloths and glasscloths in white checked with blue, red or, less typically, green, are also widely sold. When period curtains cannot be found, new ones made of dress-weight ginghams or seersuckers in the same colours are perfect alternatives, since these fabrics

above A 1950s refridgerator that is flanked by period graphics creates a pleasing nostalgic ambience, a look that can be obtained with the many similar posters and trays reproduced today.

were suggested as part of the 'make-do-and-mend' spirit of World War II and its immediate after-years. That 'wiggly' trimming, ric-rac, would be an ideal finish, stitched along the top edge of a deep hem. Search for that must-have item of the period, a radio, to authenticate the look – it is still easy to find attractive examples.

Collecting kitchen furniture and objects of this era has an additional advantage, since your key pieces can be complemented by many easily found packaged foods and other household products. Plastic bottles with symmetrical shapes are very likely to have been developed in the mid-twentieth century. As to labelling, there are 'period pieces' in every section of the supermarket. In the USA, Comet powdered cleanser, Arm & Hammer baking soda, Del Monte tinned fruit, Nestle's chocolate chips, Oreo cookies, A1 steak sauce, French's mustard and Campbell's basic soups and, in the UK, Colman's mustard, Heinz baked beans, Ovaltine and Marmite are among those that have changed but little or not at all in the past 50 or so years. Many of these are also available elsewhere. A surefire clue to the older 'authentic' labels is the presence of a registration symbol next to the identifying image, as can be found on the cylindrical cardboard containers of Sun-Maid raisins, Morton's salt and Quaker Oats. Minor details may have changed, but the overall appearance makes such bright packaging – predominantly red, navy, bright green and yellows – just right for open shelves such as line the Burgess-Newman kitchen. Once their original contents have been consumed, the lidded cardboard containers offer the extra plus of being able to hold other things. Even if the containers are not original, thinking of new ways to use them is a thoroughly 'in-period' pastime.

comforting obsessions

Simon Gee

It is often the most extreme examples of collecting that reveal the connections between obsessions, life histories and the way we construct emotional security by using meaning-laden objects in our interiors. Simon Gee's two-roomed flat in London's Kentish Town offers such an insight. Containing few creature comforts – there is no bed, for example – it instead provides comforts of other kinds. All problems disappear when he is absorbed in finding, restoring and arranging his objects.

When interviewed by Tim Willis in 2000, Gee admitted to being an 'unhealthy, incurable obsessive'. There is a touch of irony in his comment, however, for aside from long, liberating bicycle rides in the country, his obsessive collecting is what keeps this New Zealander sane in the midst of his scruffy, adopted urban environment. He adds constantly to what seems at first glance to be simply a jumbled array of unconnected objects. There are anatomical models, china dolls' heads, tailors' scissors, meat cleavers, sewing-thread bobbins, keys, toolmakers' callipers, ear syringes, steel shoe lasts, and skeletons, some obtained from medical suppliers

right Gee's collection sprawls across his entire living room, providing its owner with few creature comforts but great psychological satisfaction.

far right Arranging a multitude of humble objects suggests that there is something special about their origins, who made them or why they have been saved.

and others from animal road-accident victims retrieved on his country rides, or mementos of the rats that were once his pets. A clue to the connections he makes between this motley array of things is his current pet, a gerbil named Dr Faustus. The infamous story of this sixteenth-century doctor, astrologer, alchemist and philosopher has been retold in many influential versions since that time, most recently in 1993 by the great Czech filmmaker Jan Svankmajer, whom Gee admires. Svankmajer's Faust is portrayed as a kind of Everyman confronted with a tragic choice. He has to choose between expanding his knowledge even though he knows he will be punished, or spending his life in the institutionalized happiness that is promised by society. It is clear which of the paths Gee has chosen, and that a significant theme underpinning his collecting is a need to know about construction, destruction and replication, largely expressed as these impact on life. And, in a parallel to Svankmajer's Faust, his own 'punishment' is the 'inhospitable' home that results from his collecting.

The relevance of Gee's admittedly unusual rooms can be discovered in another comparison to Svankmajer. It has been said of the latter that he 'delves deeply into the darkest recesses of his being in order to uncover and portray complex, disturbing emotions and impulses that are, paradoxically, universal.' This description, by the writer

above By setting gleaming metal objects against wooden planks, Gee has emphasised their machine-made aspect.

right A collage of photocopied bills of mortality, undertaker's advertisements and funeral invitations, 'interfere with' and involve the objects placed over it.

Geoff Andrew, is equally appropriate for Gee, as both he and Svankmajer collect bones and skulls, marionettes or their approximations, moulds, knives, shoes and countless *objets trouvés*. Other more conventional objects can provide an intense connection to their previous owners or makers; this 'magical' content is simply made much clearer by the sorts of things both these men collect. Gee speaks of his interest in the intimate relationship between an object, its creator and its user, pointing to his collection of old keys as an example: 'Each of them must have taken one man a whole day to make. Today they're all stamped and you just get a bit shaved off at a heel bar.' Viewed in this way his collections seem sensible, forthright, even engaging. If his point of view seems surreal, this, too, is apt. Svankmajer, a leading member of the Czech Surrealist Group – as well as a ceramicist, puppeteer, sculptor, artist and poet – describes Surrealism as 'a psychology,

a view of the world, which poses new questions about freedom, eroticism, the subconscious, and which attracts a certain sort of people – subversive types. It offers an alternative to the ideology offered by most modern societies, and it's a great adventure; it's tried to return art, which has become representational, aesthetic, commercial, to its level of magic ritual.'

Bizarre though some of his found things might be in insolation, Gee's involvement with them as evidence of his interior life does not prevent us from seeing how these objects are brought to life by visually dramatic and challenging juxtapositions. Gleaming metal is set against textured wood; bleached bones are set against black-painted walls. Patternmaking is tried out and displayed in all manner of ways. There are conscious collections, items brought together in tightly massed groups to highlight their form and variations. As Gee says of his keys, 'A multiplicity of objects is more interesting, both for their similarities and differences.' There is, conversely, the use of a background pattern to 'involve' and 'interfere with' the objects arranged over it in a seemingly informal way, as in Gee's hall, where the wall is papered with a collage of photocopies of old engravings of bills of mortality, funeral invitations, undertaker's advertising bills, and so on. His obsession with anatomy is most evident here, but the sum total is no more disturbing than Leonardo da Vinci's early sixteenth-century drawings of cadavers. It seems right that Leonardo and Faust were contemporaries, and that Gee himself has worked as a graphic artist.

Gee's interiors are decadent in one way only: they are unified by his surrealistic exercise of the power of transformation, creating for himself a safe haven through the exclusion of the exterior world. His own interiors, in fact, are true works of art. It would be supremely fitting if one of his rare visitors were Svankmajer, whose one remaining ambition is to accomplish the uniquely individual feat of what Gee has done – to make a wonderful object out of his own house.

Today's interiors are a mature amalgam of a wide range of influences. Much in our homes is modern – indebted to developments over the past 75 or so years. Much looks back as far as the sixteenth century for its inspiration, not necessarily stylistically but in the way that we use and interpret certain basic things. That century is deemed to have given birth to the 'rational' world in which we live, different from the 'spiritual', medieval era preceding it. Yet today the spiritual and the rational are both increasingly brought to bear in interiors, just as they are in life. It appears that we are on the cusp of a new age, in which the material and spiritual may well play an equal part.

Civilization was on a similar cusp around the years of 1500. This was a time when, as Luciana Arbace has put it: '… new internal struggles, doubts, and uncertainties surfaced in man's consciousness. Europe was devastated by fierce conflicts … Arts, as interpreters of the spirit of their age, tended towards an art of twisted forms, broken lines, … sumptuous and brilliant effects, strong chromatic contrasts, and bright or metallic tonalities.' Under the same influences, 'the fantasy of decorators was unleashed. Collecting underwent a revolutionary transformation … from a private activity it became part of the exercise of power. Archeological finds, oriental products and exotic curiosities were particularly in demand – the strange and curious were placed in purpose-built show-cases or shelves.' This describes the period of Machiavelli and Michelangelo, referred to as Mannerist. The parallels between then and now are striking. Mannerists and current cultural commentators alike demonstrate a preoccupation with language, its contradictions, diversity and material expression. Michelangelo, through poetry and correspondence as well as his work, sought a unity of art, existence and salvation. We might prefer to call it a unity of beauty, personal identity and spirituality or sanity. Whatever the terminology, new mannerist interiors also communicate both who we are and who we wish to be.

Mannerism was a style that spread quickly from its roots in Italy to other European states; as it did so the sobriety of the early Renaissance gave way to a relative opulence that lastingly transformed interiors, bequeathing to us the rituals associated with more sociable houses, with their formal dining rooms, guest accommodation and clearly distinguished public and private rooms. There have been several attempts in the past to return to pre-mannerist modes of living, but none has been successful. Modernism is a case in point. In Mies van der Rohe's proclamation, 'less is more', he was referring to the space and the number of walls dividing an interior. His arguments could equally validate the medieval great hall as a model for living; it, too, contained portable, multi-functional furniture and was an 'open-plan' space used for all the activities we associate with life indoors. Yet however much Medievalism, Modernism – or Minimalism – has been proclaimed as the way forward, interiors today show much stronger inclinations towards the sociable, the strange and curious, the sumptuous. Neomannerist seems to sum up this trend.

Neomannerism puts the emphasis on effect rather than on acquisition. This term 'effect' can simultaneously mean both 'impact on the environment' and 'visual impact', depending on your individual preferences. Take your clues from your personal responses to colour, materials and shapes as inspiration; add those things that will represent your own memories and aspirations; group them in ways that will stimulate the desire to look at them in detail and to touch them. The latter also engages your visitors, which is important to consider because the term 'effect' also implies the sympathetic interaction between people, their own small world, and the things they choose to surround themselves with. These are the keys to creating interiors that are richer, more meaningful and therefore more enchantingly individual.

left The 'Glasshouse', created by architect Michael Davis for Andrew Logan, is described by its owner as an organic space, forever changing; although open plan, it is sumptuous, inviting and full of neomannerist effects.

acknowledgements

My first thanks are due to Emma Clegg, who both conceived of and edited this volume; and also to the excellent team of picture researcher Marissa Keating and designer Alison Fenton, whose combined contribution to this book was vital to its realization. Aside from their professionalism, evident in these pages, each was a delight to work with, a bonus that is greatly appreciated. Too numerous to name are the many friends and colleagues who have, over the years, shared reminiscences of interiors and comments on their homes. For corrections and additions to details of the text, however, I would like to thank Anna Buruma, John Chesshyre, Lynn Felsher, Philip Hughs, Thomas Jayne, Andrew Logan, Jackie Mayhew, Roy Robison, Treve Rosoman and Cynthia Weaver; special thanks go to my fiancé Terry McLean, who helped me keep it simple. For their contribution to the case studies, I am indebted to Philip Agee, Adrian Mibus and Sue Timney. I would also like to acknowledge the authors of the quotations opening each chapter and of the following texts mentioned in this volume. (Brackets denote subject matter.)

Luciana Arbace, 'Mannerism', *Encyclopedia of Interior Design*, ed. J Banham (London and Chicago: Fitzroy Dearborn), 1997

David Batchelor, *Chromophobia* (London: Reaktion Books), 2000

[Roberto Bergero], Barbara Stoeltie, 'Colour Therapy', *World of Interiors*, September 1998

Neil Bingham and Andrew Weaving, *Modern Retro: living with mid-century modern style* (London and New York: Ryland Peters & Small), 2000

Pierre Bourdieu, *Acts of Resistance: against the tyranny of the market* (Editions Liber-Raisons D-Agir), 1998

Akiko Busch, *Geography of Home: writings on where we live* (New York: Princeton Architectural Press) 1999

Tom Dixon, *Rethink* (London: Conran Octopus), 2000

Simon Doonan, 'Is Tony Duquette *Bonkers?' Nest*, Summer 1999

Mary Douglas and Baron Isherwood, *The World of Goods: towards an anthropology of consumption* (New York: Basic Books), 1996

Dorothy Draper *Decorating is Fun!* (New York: Doubleday, Doran & Co), 1939 and 1944

Elle Decoration issue 1, summer 1989

John Elsner and Roger Cardinal (eds.), *The Cultures of Collecting* (London: Reaktion Books) 1994

[Fun furs], *House Beautiful* 142 no.2 February 2000 page 32

[Simon Gee], Tim Willies, 'Memento Mori' *The World of Interiors*, May 2000

[Romeo Gigli], Catherine Ardouin, 'À Milan l'autre d'un couturier voyageur', *Marie-Claire Maison* May/June 2000

Malcolm Gladwell, *The Tipping Point: how little things can make a big difference* (Boston, New York & London: Little, Brown & Co), 2000

[Michael Graves], 'Classic Harmony', *Art & Antiques* April 1999

Johnny Grey, *The Art of Kitchen Design* (London: Cassell) 1994

'Victoria Hagan', Amanda Vaill, *Architectural Digest* September 2000

Sharon Hanby-Robie, *My name isn't Martha, but I can decorate my home: the real person's guide to creating a beautiful home easily and affordably* (New York: Pocket Books) 1998

[Christine Krönke], Anna Lambert, 'Independent spirit: Christine Kröncke', *idFX*, June 2000

[Sol LeWitt], Susannah M. Wilson, 'Wrapped in High Art', *Art & Antiques*, December 1999

Mary Ellen Mark, 'Souvenirs of a Career', *ARTnews* Summer 2000

Daniel Miller (ed.) *Material Cultures: Why some things matter* (University of Chicago Press) 1998

Melanie Molesworth, *Junk Style* (London: Ryland Peters and Small and New York: Stewart, Tabori & Chang), 1998

[Paloma Picasso], *Elle Decoration* issue 3, Winter 1989

'Andrée Putman by herself', *Nest* 11, Winter 2000–2001

Robert B. Reich, 'The Choice Fetish: blessings and curses of a market place', in *Civilization* (Library of Congress), Aug/Sep 2000

Paul Robertson, 'Medical Quartet', *RSA Journal vcxlviii* no. 5494 (Royal Society of Arts, London), Third Quarter 2000

[Nina Saunders], 'Purity and Fear', *Make* 74, February/March 1997

Carol Sama Sheehan, *Mary Emmerling's American Country Details* (New York: Clarkson Potter) 1997

[Laura Stoddart], *World of Interiors*, November 1999

James Surowiecki in Thomas L. Friedman, *The Lexus and the Olive Tree: Understanding Globalization* [1999] (New York: Anchor Books), 2000

[Jan Svankmajer] Geoff Andrew, 'A Faust Buck', *Time Out*, September 1994

Louise Taylor (ed.), *Decadence? Views from the edge of the century* [playing cards] (London: Crafts Council Gallery), 199

Robert Venturi, *Complexity and Contradiction in Architecture* (New York: Museum of Modern Art), 1966

Margaret Visser, *The Rituals of Dinner* (New York: Penguin) 1993

[Mary Rose Young], 'A shade more daring', *Metropolitan Home* (UK) October 1990

To Terry

First published in 2001 by
Conran Octopus Limited
A part of Octopus Publishing Group
2–4 Heron Quays
London E14 4JP

www.conran-octopus.co.uk

ISBN 1 84091 191 3

Text © Conran Octopus 2001
Design and layout
© Conran Octopus 2001

Publishing Director: Lorraine Dickey
Commissioning Editor: Emma Clegg
Editorial Assistant: Lara McCann
Proofreader: Libby Willis
Indexer: Helen Snaith

Creative Director: Leslie Harrington
Designer: Alison Fenton
Picture Research: Marissa Keating

Production Director: Zoe Fawcett
Senior Production Controller: Manjit Sihra

British Library Cataloguing-in-Publication Data
A catalogue record for this book is available from the British Library

Printed and bound in China

picture credits

The publisher would like to thank the following photographers and agencies for their kind permission to reproduce the photographs in this book:

1 Luke White/The Interior Archive (Sparkle Moore); 2 James Mortimer/World of Interiors; 4 left Steve Dalton/Red Cover; 4 right Jan Baldwin/Narratives (Niki de Saint Phalle); 4 above centre Earl Carter/Belle Magazine; 5 left Christie's Images (Designer: Miles van der Rohe); 5 right Luke White/The Interior Archive (Sparkle Moore); 5 centre Simon Upton/The Interior Archive (Designer: Kit Kemp);6 Dennis Gilbert/National Trust Photo Library (Designer: Goldfinger); 8 Luke White/The Interior Archive; 10 left Bill Batten/National Trust Photo Library; 10-11 Derry Moore (Nest magazine); 11 Solvi Dos Santos; 12 Fritz von der Schulenberg/Interior Archive; 13 Solvi Dos Santos; 14-15 Andrew Twort/Red Cover; 16-17 Versace; 17 Modus Publicity (Benneton); 18 Melvyn Vincent Photography; 19 right Courtesy of Apple Macintosh; 19 below Simon Upton/The Interior Archive; 20 Ronald Grant Archive/Orion; 20-21 Steve Dalton/Red Cover; 21 right Ronald Grant Archive/LWT; 22 James Mortimer/World of Interiors; 23 Simon Kenny/Belle 1994/Arcaid; 23 left Atelier Mendini; 24 Janet Stoyle; 25 Richard Barnes/Nest Magazine; 26 Anthea Simms/Camera Press; 26 above Courtesy of Sadie Coles (Artist: Sarah Lucas); 27 below Red Saunders (Designer: Nina Saunders); 28 Brian Harrison/Red Cover; 28-29 Tom Mannion/World of Interiors; 30 Gerd Verschoor/Verne Fotografie; 31 Mary Annella Frank; 32 Luke White/The Interior Archive; 34 P.Van Robaeys/Narratives; 36 William Waldron/Archard and Associates; 37 Wayne Vincent/The Interior Archive; 38 Paul Ryan/International Interiors; 38 right Richard Bryant/Arcaid; 39 Henry Wilson/The Interior Archive; 40-41 Solvi Dos Santos; 42 above G Pesce/Verne Fotografie; 42 below Christie's Images (Designer: William Morris / Painter: Rossetti); 43 Luke White/Axiom Photographic Agency; 44-45 Robert Harding; 45 Fritz von der Schulenburg/The Interior Archive; 46 Andreas Von Einsiedel/National Trust Photo Library; 47 left Tim Beddow/The Interior Archive; 47 right Richard Waite/Arcaid; 48 Clive Frost; 48 right Jan Baldwin/Narratives; 49 John Edward Linden/Arcaid (Designer: Andrew Logan); 50 Andreas Von Einsiedel/Red Cover; 51 Jean-Louis Garnell/Nest magazine; 52 left Gilles/Verne Fotografie; 52-53 Nicholas Kane/Arcaid (Designer: Julie Verhoeven); 53 Joel Laiter/World of Interiors; 54-57 Rene and Barbara Stoeltie; 58 Luke White/The Interior Archive; 60 Solvi Dos Santos; 60 left Guy Obijn (Pieter Backer); 60 right Anthony Oliver (Designer: Dai Rees); 62 left Luke White/The Interior Archive; 62 right Andrew Wood/The Interior Archive; 63 Solvi Dos Santos; 64 Brian Harrison/Red Cover; 65 left Luke White/The Interior Archive; 65 right Solvi Dos Santos; 66 Josie Hilton-Barber/Narratives; 66 left Paul Ryan/International Interiors; 67 Luke White/The Interior Archive; 68 left Henry Wilson/The Interior Archive; 68 right Solvi Dos Santos; 69 Antoine Bootz; 70 Edina van der Wyck/The Interior Archive; 71 Henry Wilson/The Interior Archive; 72 Noelle Hoeppe; 73 left Neville Trickett/Saint Verde; 74 left Fritz von der Schulenburg/The Interior Archive; 74 right Fernando Bengoechea/The Interior Archive; 75 Wayne Vincent/The Interior Archive; 76 Jan Baldwin/Narratives (Nikki St de Phalle); 76-77 Nicholas Kane/Arcaid (Designer: Julie Verhoenen); 77 Jan Baldwin/Narratives (Jacopo Foggini); 78-81 Jim Goldberg (Nest Magazine); 82 Luke White/The Interior Archive; 84 Brian Harrison/Red Cover; 85 Jean-Louis Garnell/Nest magazine (owner: Jacques Grange); 86 Clive Frost (Owner: Miranda Rhys Williams); 87 Andreas Von Einsiedel/The National Trust Photo Library; 88 Fritz von der Schulenburg/The Interior Archive; 88-89 Richard Barnes/Nest Magazine (Designer: Morris Lapidus); 89 Solvi Dos Santos; 90 Petrina Tinslay/Belle Magazine; 91 Christie's Images (Designer: Miles van der Rohe -1929); 91 right Fritz von der Schulenburg/The Interior Archive; 92 Henry Wilson/The Interior Archive; 92-93 Fernando Bengoechea/The Interior Archive; 93 Geffrye Museum; 94 The Kobal Collection/MGM (Leonard Rossiter); 95 Richard Bryant/Arcaid (Lighting by Zumtobel Staff AG); 96 Ken Hayden/Red Cover (Owner: David Gill); 97 Deidi von Schaewen; 98 Henry Wilson/The Interior Archive; 98 right Winfried Heinze/Red Cover (Rolsyn Jackson); 99 James Mortimer/World of Interiors; 100-101 Henry Wilson/The Interior Archive (Designer: Mibus); 101 Habitat UK (Designer: Robin Day); 102-103 Henry Wilson/The Interior Archive (Designer: Mibus); 104 Luke White/The Interior Archive (Owner: Noisha Crosland); 106 Winterthur Museum; 108 left Jonathan Bailey/English Heritage Photo Library; 108-109 Christopher Simon Sykes/The Interior Archive; 109 Andreas von Einsiedel/National Trust Photo Library; 110 Nigel Spalding; 110 right Geoffery Frosh/National Trust Photo Library (Ayot St Lawrence); 111 Luke White/The Interior Archive (Syon House); 112 Fernando Bengoechea/The Interior Archive (Property: South Beach); 113 left Brian Harrison/Red Cover; 113 right Andreas Von Einsiedel/National Trust Photo Library (Calke Abbey); 114 Anne Garde; 115 Jacques Dirand/World of Interiors; 116 Cora/Marie Claire Maison (Stylist: C.Pench); 117 left Steve Wright/The Interior Archive; 117 right Henry Wilson/The Interior Archive (Designer: Gizzar Giray); 118 Henry Wilson/The Interior Archive (Artist: Steve Wright); 118-119 Jan Baldwin / Narratives (Josie Hilton-Barber); 119 right Verne Fotografie; 120 Mark Bolton/Red Cover; 121 Brian Harrison/Red Cover; 122-123 Andreas von Einsiedel; 123 Courtesy of Timoney Fowler; 124-125 Andrew Wood/The Interior Archive (Designer: Timoney Fowler); 126 Edina van der Wyck/The Interior Archive (Owner: Ojeda); 128 Simon Brown/The Interior Archive; 128-129 Andrew Twort/Red Cover (Nathelie Hembro); 129 Andreas von Einsiedel/National Trust Photo Library (Ickworth Museum); 130 Simon Upton/The Interior Archive (Lulu Guiness); 131 Jason Schmidt/Tom Booth/Nest Magazine; 132 left Verne Fotografie (Paula Levine); 132-133 Fritz von der Schulenberg/The Interior Archive (Designer: Adelheld von der Schulenburg); 134 Lucinda Lambton/Arcaid (David Harrison); 135 Edina van der Wyck/Conde Nast Publications Ltd; 136 Andreas von Einsiedel/Red Cover; 136-137 Brian Harrisson/Red Cover; 137-Fritz von der Schulenberg/The Interior Archive (Florist: Barry Fergurson); 138 left Fritz von der Schulenberg/The Interior Archive (Antique dealer: John Russel); 138-139 Fritz von der Schulenburg/The Interior Archive (Architect: Jorg Marguard); 139 Andrew Wood/The Interior Archive; 140 Fritz von der Schulenburg/The Interior Archive (Designer: Jacques Grange); 141 Nigel Spalding; 142-143 Fritz von der Schulenberg/The Interior Archive (Owner: Circus Roncalli); 143 left Ikea; 144-145 Fritz von der Schulenberg/The Interior Archive (Owner: Circus Roncalli); 146 -149 Anthony Oliver (Terry Burgess); 150-151 Simon Upton/World of Interiors (Martin Gee); 151 Simon Upton/World of Interiors (Martin Gee); 152 Simon Upton/World of Interiors (Martin Gee); 154 John Edward Linden/Arcaid (Andrew Logan)

Every effort has been made to trace the copyright holders, architects and designers and we apologise in advance for any unintentional omissions, and would be pleased to insert the appropriate acknowledgement in any subsequent publication.